D0992614

Becoming a Teacher
A Lifelong Journey

PEDAGOGICAL BOOKS by A. F. ADA

IN ENGLISH
*** A Magical Encounter: Latino Children's
Literature in the Classroom
* My Books: My life
* Dolores Salvador: maestra de maestras**
IN SPANISH
*** Iniciación Literaria
* Oír y Narrar
* Ver y describir**

co-authored with F. ISABEL CAMPOY

IN ENGLISH
*** Authors in the Classroom: A
Transformative
Education Experience
* Spanish Literacy: Strategies for Young
Learners**
IN SPANISH
*** Ayudando a nuestros hijos
* Está linda la mar. Para entender la
poesía y usarla en el aula
* Música amiga. Aprender cantando
* Palabra amiga. Domine su idioma
* La fascinante historia de la lengua
española
* Guía para padres y maestros de niños
bilingües** [with Colin Baker]

Alma Flor Ada

Becoming a Teacher
A Lifelong Journey

mariposa
San Rafael, California

mariposa
Transformative Education Services
San Rafael, California

ISBN 978-1-938061-96-7

To my son
Miguel Zubizarreta-Ada
and his wife Denise
whose lives
are incomparable gifts
and their children,
Tim, Samantha, Victoria and Nick,
constant sources of hope.

Alma Flor Ada

With appreciation to all those
who, in multiple locations,
through sixty-four years,
have accompanied me
in the unending journey of becoming
a teacher
making it meaningful and joyful
with their sincerity,
their creativity,
and their honest reflections.

Always grateful.

CUBAN EDUCATORS' LEGACY

Félix Varela
[La Habana, Cuba, 1788 - San Agustín, FL, 1853]
> According to José de la Luz y Caballero,
> *Varela taught us to think.*

José Antonio Saco
[Bayamo, Cuba, 1797-Barcelona, España, 1879]
> *Public instruction is the strongest basis*
> *to support the happiness of nations.*

José de la Luz y Caballero
[La Habana, Cuba, 1800-1862]
> *Teach anyone can do; educate, only*
> *someone who is a living gospel.*

Rafael María de Mendive y Daumy
[La Habana, Cuba, 1821-1875]
> *How do you want me to say in a few lines all the goodness and originality of that lover of beauty, who wanted it as much in literature as in life, and who never wrote anything but the truth in his heart and the sufferings of his homeland?*
> José Martí about his teacher
> Rafael María de Mendive

José Martí
[La Habana, 1853- Dos Ríos, Oriente, 1895]

To do is the best way to make a statement.
It is preferable the wellbeing of many than the
opulence of a few.
The only autograph of any value is that written
by a person's actions.

María Luisa Dolz y Arango
[La Habana, 1854- 1928]

You have left, but your creation remains. Your mission as an educator is fulfilled. You show us the right path, giving us examples of hard work, perseverance and generosity. Your amazing activity, your equanimity your love for justice are norms we follow with devotion.

Dolores Salvador about her
teacher María Luisa Dolz

Dolores Salvador Méndez de Lafuente
[Camagüey, Cuba, 1887- 1943]

Our school is a school of joy and spontaneity. Our students are our friends. We do not sow pain and thus we gather love. We respect the right to happiness which is childhood's right.

Like her teacher, Dolores devoted her
life to equality in education.

9

Acknowledgement

My life has been blessed by the presence of extraordinary educators, beginning with my grandparents, parents, uncles, and aunts.

The names of my teachers, including the students who allow me the experience of becoming an educator became in turn my teachers, would be a long list. Some are recognized individually through the narrative and in the section *Gratitude*, but I would like to state here my how grateful I am to all. The list of the dissertations is an acknowledgement of the doctoral students who gave me the opportunity to learn with them as I guided their research.

The last 25 years of this journey have been enriched by sharing them with Isabel Campoy. Her positive outlook of life and her commitment to create a better world by promoting voice and empowerment deserve both my admiration and my gratitude.

This journey would not have been possible without the kindness, support, generosity, understanding and love of my children, Rosalma, Alfonso, Miguel and Gabriel Zubizarreta Ada, who now, in this retrospective view, I must acknowledge as my most constant teachers.

Contents

Presentation

Enseñar puede cualquiera,
educar, solo quien sea un Evangelio vivo.
José de la Luz y Caballero

My long life journey has had a very clear goal: to become a true teacher, deserving of the privilege of guiding my students in their own pursue of learning.

The journey started very early when unforeseen circumstances made me responsible at the age of eighteen for teaching two college courses at Loretto Heights College in Denver, Colorado where I was a freshman. This unusual experience will be described on the next chapter.

The practice continued one more year, in similar circumstances of teaching in exchange for my tuition while a sophomore at Barry College, in Florida. Later, while pursuing a doctorate degree, at the Pontificia Universidad

Católica del Perú, in Lima, I found myself a high school teacher, in front of students barely a handful of years younger than me.

My own experiences as a student had been very varied. During the primary grades in my hometown of Camagüey, Cuba, I studied in five very different Elementary Schools. Four were private schools, two were sponsored by American missionaries but both were of different denominations, two were Cuban and very different from each other. Only one of the five was a Cuban public school, and there I learned what a true teacher can bring to a child's life when learning becomes joyful, in contrast to the other four schools that had left mostly painful memories.

In that public school, the demonstration school for the Normal School for Teachers, I was able to experience from my extraordinary sixth grade teacher, Dr. Rosita Peyrellade, that teaching could be meaningful, sustaining, and inspiring. Previous experiences had taught me that it could also be dreadful. Since I do not believe that the teachers who made my elementary school experiences so miserable were necessarily bad persons, it became obvious that being a true teacher was not necessarily easy or a given.

My admiration and gratitude for the teachers that later enriched my life led me to try to continue learning from their example, knowing that teaching held great promises, but that to fulfill them constant awareness was needed.

In Perú I taught at two schools, the Abraham Lincoln Bilingual School and the Alexander von Humboldt Trilingual School. And I will be forever grateful to the students in both these schools who helped me begin to learn to be a teacher. They continue to hold a very special place in my heart and I feel blessed that I have been able to reconnect with many of them who continue deserving my gratitude and admiration.

For thirty-four years, I was a university professor in the United States, first as an Associate Professor at Emory University, teaching doctoral seminars of Spanish and Latin American Literature. Then, as Full Professor at Mercy College of Detroit, where I taught undergraduate courses in Spanish and Spanish and Latin American Literature and developed the first bilingual teacher training program in the state of Michigan. My longest teaching experience has taken place at the doctoral program in International Multicultural Education at the University of San Francisco.

Along these full time positions, many summer I taught at different universities, Tufts University, in Medford, MA; Associate Colleges of the Midwest, in Chicago; University of Texas at El Paso; St. Thomas University in Houston, Texas; the University of Guam; the Complutense University in Madrid and the Fundación José Ortega y Gasset also in Madrid and I have given seminars, workshops and presentations to teachers in multiple conferences and school districts. Each one of these settings allowed me to continue searching for ways to improve my own teaching.

At the University of San Francisco, teaching professionals working to obtain a doctoral degree offered on intensive week-ends, presented unique challenges and possibilities to reflect about learning processes. Several of those doctoral students have become great friends.

While teaching and guiding students in the process of researching and writing their dissertations was my primary occupation, my love for literature led to a career as a writer of fiction and non-fiction for both children and adults.

The awareness of the power of language, the benefits of bilingualism and plurilinguism and the detriments of monolingual policies led me to be a constant advocate of bilingual education and dual language instruction.

The oppression suffered by people of color, minorities, and those living in economic poverty and marginalized conditions, led me to a life of activism on behalf of social justice.

These diverse passions have informed one another in a variety of ways: My love for literature as a teaching tool inspired *A Magical Encounter: The Use of Children's Literature in the Classroom* a pedagogical book on the effective role of children's literature in the classroom (Ada, 2003, 2016) and *Está linda la mar. Para entender la poesía y usarla en el aula* a book on the use of poetry in the classroom, coauthored with F. Isabel Campoy (Ada and Campoy, 2015).

My concern for having parents be authentic partners in their children education became the topic of several articles, mentioned in the references, the co-authorship with Isabel Campoy of the book *Ayudando a nuestros hijos* and with Isabel and Colin Baker of *Guía para padres y maestros de niños bilingües*.

The joy I experienced writing led to authoring many books for children, and two novels, a memoir, and two books of poetry for adult readers. Since writing was something I did in my own time, after taking care of my responsibilities as a professor, I have never quite thought of me as a professional author, but rather as an educator who writes.

My firm believe in the value of bilingualism and the limitations imposed by monolinguism, and the dream that all children be able to maintain and develop their home language, along with my passionate love for my Spanish language, that I call *mi matria*, "the house of my Being," paraphrasing Heidegger, led to the writing of children's literature in Spanish, of materials to develop reading in Spanish, and in collaboration with Isabel Campoy, pedagogical materials as well as a history of the Spanish language.

The concern for migrant farm-working families led to several family literacy projects designed to empower language-minority parents by using children's literature as a springboard for meaningful home-school interactions. The one developed in Pájaro Valley under the auspices of Alfonso Anaya, then Migrant Education Director in that district (Ada, 1988), has been extensively studied and replicated.

The work to promote that parents and children would create their own books, developed further into *Authors in the Classroom: A Transformative Education Process*, a process for encouraging parents, teachers, and children to become authors of their own stories, co-developed with Isabel Campoy (Ada & Campoy, 2004). The collaboration of my daughter Rosalma Zubizarreta contributed to further develop the anti-bias component of this process as presented in the book.

Isabel and I offered courses, workshops and presentations on the process of authorship conducive not only to encouraging written expression but also to the development of critical awareness. And we saw the process having as much impact in Micronesia as in Bulgaria, in Mexico as in the Czech Republic, in Micronesia as in Puerto Rico, and multiple other areas in the world.

Yet, it was only when I retired from the university, that I found the opportunity to write in greater depth about my own journey as an author and an educator, to reflect aloud on the praxis of learning alongside my students and sharing in their journeys of discovery and research.

For this I am grateful to the *Journal for Latinos in Education*, and in particular to Dr. Enrique Murillo. It was due to his invitation to share my educational life that I first took the time to organize my reflections on what I have learned over the years as a university professor, and to describe the learning community that I have been privileged to co-create with my students.

I wish to thank my daughter, Rosalma Zubizarreta, for her insightful and supportive collaboration on the first version of these reflections, published as an article "A Lifetime of Learning to Teach" in the *Journal of Latinos and Education.*

The encouragement of my son Miguel Zubizarreta Ada made me decide to revisit that article and expand it to become this book. Gracias, Miguel, for once again encouraging me to do just a little bit more.

Lucas Valley
San Rafael, California
December, 2018 – February, 2020

I. Preparing to Become a Teacher

While teaching has been my professional occupation throughout my life, I did not become a teacher by formally studying Education.

When after obtaining a PhD in Literature from the *Pontificia Universidad Católica del Perú* I discovered that in order to teach at a School of Education I would need a PhD in Education, I registered for such a program, at the *Universidad de San Marcos*, in Lima, knowing that many of the courses I had already completed for the PhD in Literature would be transferable as it would, at a personal level, my experience in research.

My studies of Education did not last very long. I completed by examination the basic

First Year courses, but because I moved immediately after to the United States, I basically never attended any classes specifically about education.

But learning is not limited to what is offered in specific courses and I had an extraordinary opportunity to learn a great deal about education through my family environment, my initial experiential circumstances at *Loretto Heights College* and *Barry College* [now *Barry University*] and my years of teaching at the *Abraham Lincoln* and *Alexander von Humboldt Schools*.

We do not know as yet how much of our ancestors' knowledge and experiences may be carried on by our DNA. I certainly have an ample legacy from educators.

My maternal great-grandparents, Lorenzo Lafuente Garoña, from Ameyugo, Burgos, Spain, a writer, and Virginia Rubio Sierra, from Madrid, were both educators who owned a small private school, the *Colegio San José*, in Madrid.

Their eldest son, my grandfather, Medardo Lafuente Rubio, poet and journalist, was a Professor of Spanish Literature and of French at the *Instituto de Segunda Enseñanza de Camagüey*.

My maternal grandmother, Dolores (Lola) Salvador Méndez, from Camagüey, Cuba, did study to become a teacher at the *Colegio María Luisa Dolz* where she was Valedictorian of her graduating class. Studying with María Luisa Dolz, a committed feminist and progressive educator was a privilege that my grandmother recognized not only in her writings but in her own praxis as an innovative socially conscious and highly effective teacher. She passed on this legacy to her own daughters, my mother and her sisters.

Together Medardo and Lola administered for some time a private school, *Colegio El Porvenir*, and later founded their own *Colegio Lafuente-Salvador*, a combination day and boarding secular school, for girls and boys, housed in their own home, the colonial Quinta Simoni, inherited by Lola

27

from her father, don Federico Salvador Arias. The memories shared by my mother and aunts, themselves students of that innovative school, where many classes were conducted outdoors, were very much reminiscent of Louise May Alcott's descriptions of the school in *Jo's Boys*.

At some point, after the basic education of their five children was completed, the *Colegio Lafuente-Salvador* was closed. My grandfather focused his teaching at the Instituto where he was highly regarded, and my grandmother went up to fulfill her dream of creating the first public night school for working women in the province of Camagüey.

My childhood was enriched by listening about my grandparents, who died when I was still very little, but left indelible memories, and hearing numerous expressions of gratitude from people, including some of my own teachers, who had been their students.

But family stories about education were not limited to my grandparents. My oldest aunt Dr. Virginia Lafuente became a teacher and later a Professor of Education at the Normal School for Teachers, first in Camagüey, later in La Habana. My aunt Mireya, who also had a Ph.D. in Education, and who had studied with the Ballet Folklórico de México, became a professor of Physical Education and Folkloric Dances, and my aunt Lolita was a Home Economics teacher. Their experiences were shared and commented in family gatherings.

This repertoire of teaching anecdotes and practices was highly enriched when my mother accepted to offer boarding to three young women, from the city of Bayamo, who wanted to study in Camagüey since in Bayamo there was no Normal Schools for Teachers. Belkis and Aleida studied to become elementary teachers, Tati, a gifted pianist, went to the specialized Normal School for Kindergarten Teachers, which required musical knowledge and the ability to play the piano, since music was considered an integral part of kindergarten education.

In our family, meal times, both at lunch and dinner, were occasions for interesting conversations. The experiences of these three young women and their learning became daily topics.

The education of teachers in Cuba during the 1950s included both theory and practice. Beginning on their first year, students were required to prepare demonstration lessons that they carried on in the *Escuela Anexa*, or Demonstration School. Throughout the year all students would teach lessons on different subjects in different grades. Their classmates would observe and later critique their performance which would also be evaluated by the classroom teacher and the school Principal. Later they would become student teachers for several days on the different grade level classrooms.

Although at that time my mother was not professionally an educator, but an accountant, she was an inborn teacher, one of the best I have ever encountered. She could not pass on the opportunity of encouraging and coaching the three young women. While Belkis was rather self-assured, Aleida and Tati welcomed the encouragement. The future kindergarten teacher was particularly shy, and at the beginning would turn crimson red and had difficulty containing the tears. But my mother gentle support, sprinkled with some humor, helped her conquer her shyness.

My mother made suggestions, shared her creativity with them, and encouraged them to be daring and original. She listened several times to their presentations and the gentleness and sensitiveness with which she made comments was also for me a model of how the efforts of students ought to be received.

Needless to say, their performance was outstanding and they received high praise every time, while I internalized that in my mother's eyes, every instance could be an opportunity to teach and teaching must be done with creativity, with a determination of making the content as attractive and interesting as possible, incorporating art and originality, and always being sensitive to the students' needs and feelings.

In 1955, when I graduated from the *Instituto de Segunda Enseñanza de Camagüey* I was offered a working scholarship at *Loretto Heights College* in Denver, Colo. through the generous efforts of the librarian of the US Information Services, Yolanda Faggioni, who had received that same scholarship a few years before. In that pre-technological era, the purpose of the scholarship was to have a native-speaker assist in the Spanish Department as a model of authentic Spanish. One of the two Spanish professors was very knowledgeable about the language grammar, the Hispanic culture and literatures, but was not a fluent speaker.

For a couple of days before the beginning of classes I was tutored by the sister of Loretto that I was supposed to assist on what would be expected of me: I was to assume the role as a "living language laboratory" a rather simple task. But the very last vacation evening the gentle nun had a stroke and was rushed to the hospital. I was asked to substitute her and handle the first class on my own.

I thought the best beginning would be to assure the students on how easy it would be to learn Spanish and to demonstrate by showing them they could sound out any text written in Spanish, regardless of whether they knew the text meaning.

Having struggled, as most of those who learn English as a second language, with the large number of vowels sounds and what to me seemed very arbitrary pronunciation [**a** of *acorn* is not the same as **a** of *apple*] and sometimes **e** can be mute! I believed I would be giving the students the great news that in Spanish there are only 5 consistent vowels sounds.

Because in Spanish both **b** and **v** are pronounced /b/ I kept insisting in my limited English that Spanish was very easy to learn because, after all, it had only five "bowels." Throughout the class, the students erupted in laughter every time I repeated the same statement.

I must confess that their laughter did not really bothered me. At the time, I had not developed the awareness I later acquired of the dangers of ethnocentrism. In my limited view of the world, my vision of the people of the United States was very simplistic and rather stereotypic based on the tourists that dared to walk through our cities dressed in garish colors and wearing shorts, and had no better sense than exposing themselves to the tropical sun until they looked like roasted lobsters. Consequently, it was not surprising they could laugh merrily at the fact of learning that a language has five consistent vowels.

It took me some time to find out that the students laughter that day had been directed at me, fortunately by then we had established joyful classes, where, trying to imagine how my mother would have acted, I used songs, poems, traditional sayings, jokes and personal sharing to make the learning of the language vivid and engaging and the students were becoming fluent in the language and interested in Hispanic culture.

2. Creative Reading and Dialogue Methodology

While teaching at Mercy College in Detroit, at a time when Bilingual Education was beginning to be a strong educational movement, I was approached by a Spanish publisher who invited me to create a reading program in Spanish.

Santillana Publishing had made a similar invitation which I had declined because the offer required that I move to New York and write the materials at their office. While creating a Spanish reading series to support bilingual education was an exciting idea, I wanted to do it in addition to, not instead of, teaching.

A few years earlier, in Perú, I had developed a reading series, which I named

Edad de Oro in tribute to the children's magazine of that name, created by José Martí, which has been recognized as the beginning of Latin American children's literature.

The reading series *Edad de Oro* was an immediate success. At that time, in the 1960s Peruvian teachers made personally the choice of the teaching materials they wanted to use and the parents purchased the books indicated by the teacher. While some publishing houses with a long tradition of creating elementary text books had a selling force that made contacts with schools and teachers to promote their books. The publisher of the *Edad de Oro*, which up to then had only published college and high school materials, was not expecting initially much success from these and had decided to make only a small printing, and to save on the cost by not print all pages in color, but only some of them. He had the books placed in book stores and made no special effort to publicize them. To his great surprise, as well as mine, the complete edition was immediately sold out and he had to print another run and this time printed all the illustrations in color.

It was most rewarding to know that the books were being individually chosen by hundreds of teachers and even more rewarding whenever I saw, whether while riding home in the school bus through Lima or while walking in my neighborhood, children sitting on their door steps, or on a bench park, reading one of *Edad de Oro* books.

To create these books, I had followed the syllabic approach but had paid special attention to content and language of the texts. Staying away of the preachy and many times boringly moralizing materials which plagued many of the reading series of the time, *Edad de Oro* was rich in poetry, folklore, and stories. The non-fiction sections that needed to be present to satisfy the curriculum requirements like Home, School, Study, Nation, Civic Life, Responsibility, etc. were reduced to a paragraph of child appropriate and gentle text to open each section and then the expected information and values were presented through the stories and poetry selections that made most of the content of the books.

Following the inspiration of Martí and other excellent Latin American authors like Gabriela Mistral, Alfonsina Storni, German Berdiales, Amado Nervo, I strived to create a prose that would be musical and appealing, sometimes humorous and always engaging. I tried out the selections first with my own children and the children of friends, and then, obtained the permission from the *Colegio Alexander von Humboldt* where I taught high school courses to read and comment the selections with the students at the various elementary class levels.

Creating a reading series to be used in the United States in bilingual programs seemed like a much more challenging process, especially since in the United States there seemed to be such controversies about the best ways of teaching reading.

I began by trying to read as much as I possibly could of what had been written about the teaching of reading. While some of the reading was fascinating, most of it was painfully boring.

I will always remember the moment when I said to myself that I needed to pause on the reading and do some personal reflection. After all, I am not a very skilled person in many areas yet there is one to which I have devoted more time than to any other, and that is precisely reading. And I felt I could think of myself as a competent reader.

What had my life as a constant reader, someone who would always carry a book, who never lost the opportunity to read, for whom books had been so important, had taught me about reading?

The first point that became clear to me was that the principle of "teaching how to read" could be as ineffectual as much of what I saw in "teaching a foreign language" in contrast to facilitating language acquisition and facilitating the acquisition of reading skills.

This, of course, lead to a very basic question: if we are to facilitate the acquisition of reading skills, what is truly reading?

The answer would have a profound impact on my life from that moment onwards.

Most of what I had been reading dealt with how to ascertain that children can repeat what is written on the page... that they could sound out the words, write them if they were dictated, and answer the fundamental questions of who, what, when, where, that would allow to verify that the child has "read" the text. That verification could be turned into numbers for grades and statistics.

But it was apparent that mastering those skills did not necessarily create the joyful avid readers that I had been, that my own children were. And I could but conclude that being able to repeat what a text said, while an important skill, was **not** truly reading.

What else happens when an effective reader approaches a text? What follows the immediate decoding of the information?

A true reader does not stop at knowing what the text says, because concurrently to reading the information, the reader, as a human being, has emotional reactions to what the text communicates. A text can awaken interest or empathy, it may create surprise and disbelief, inspire sadness or pleasure, grief and commiseration or joy and enthusiasm.

The reader, focused on the information, may be unaware or unconscious to these feelings, perhaps until later. Nevertheless, these internal responses are an essential part of the reading act.

Mature, aware readers will maintain a dialogue, albeit silent, with the text: questions will arise as the reader relates the content to previous experiences. Do the information on the text corroborates the reader's previous experiences; does it enrich, challenge or contradict them?

Readers with social justice awareness will reflect on the text premises: do they represent all human beings; do they exclude some and benefit others? What would be the consequences if the text premises were to be universally adopted? What if they would be opposed?

No matter if what is being read is a personal letter, a newspaper article, a poem, a novel, a scientific thesis, whatever the genre and content; **true reading is a dialogue between reader and text**. This is why different readers will respond differently to the same text.
If we are going to educate for empowerment, to foster critical and responsible attitudes, I proposed to look at reading as a process that would go beyond the mere repetition of what the text says.

The name *Creative Reading* seems appropriate to indicate not that the initial content of the text would be modified but rather that the dialogue maintained between reader and text could lead to creative actions.

While the dialogue maintained with the text by experienced readers happens in an organic integrated matter, it seemed beneficial to present the process broken down into four phases, described below.

1. Descriptive Phase

The process begins with the understanding of what the text says. This is where most initial reading process begins, and unfortunately where most end. The reader knows the *who, what, when, where* described in the text. Sometimes *why* is added to this stage, but only when the why is of an obvious nature.

> *In the process of guiding a dialogue about the text, the traditional* **Who? What? When? Where?** *and* **Why?** *questions, in a form appropriate to the reader's maturity may be asked to ascertain the literal meaning of the text has been understood.*

2. Personal Interpretive Phase

The reader becomes aware of the personal reactions to the text, the feelings and emotions it may be inspiring. Furthermore, the reader begins the contrast with previously held beliefs and opinions, or with the previous related knowledge and experiences.

The reading may be satisfying because it provides information previously unknown, or it may challenge the level of knowledge or expertise of the reader, it also may become unacceptable or unreliable, if it ignores or contradict experiences of which the reader is very aware.

When the dialogue is conducted orally with the students this moment is of maximum importance, because it is the opportunity to validate their previous knowledge and experiences as much as to make them aware of their own role as reader.

Questions like:
  ➤ *Have you ever known someone like this character?*

> ➢ *Have you ever been in a situation like this?*
> ➢ *Have your experiences been similar or different from the ones described here?*

And also, after the previous ones have been explored, of the nature of:

> ➢ *How does this make you feel? Why?*

3. Critical Anti-bias Reflective Phase

The mature responsible reader at this point would be evaluating the text for accuracy and moral values.

A classroom dialogue will suggest a discussion of the implications of what is being read, in an age appropriate language and from a multicultural and anti-bias perspective.

While at some levels a question like *"Is this applicable to all people?"* could be acceptable, at others, the questions about characters may be more of the nature of:

> ➢ *Do you think all families behave this way?*
> ➢ *Do you think everyone is represented here?*

45

> ➤ *Are all represented fairly?*
> ➤ *Are your family and community included?*
> ➤ *Are all characters treated with equal respect?*

The dialogue concerning values beliefs and principles underlying the text may be initiated with questions like:

> ➤ *What would happen if everyone acted this way?*
> ➤ *Would these ideas bring about harmony, respect, peaceful interaction, solidarity? Will they benefit everyone equally?*

4. Creative Phase: Transformative, Liberating, Promoting Social Justice

The furthermost value of reading, while done in a reflective manner, is that beyond giving us information and/or enjoyment, it gives us tools to be more constructive, it empowers us to modify our reality.

It is important to encourage a dialogue which fully develops the awareness of this empowerment:

> *After reading this text, what will you do when you are faced with a similar situation?*
> *What do you know now that gives you strength or courage for your future actions?*

It will not be necessary to follow these steps for too long before they become an internalized practice and the dialogue can move quickly to the Critical and Creative Phases.

The Reading Program *Hagamos caminos* {Let's Open New Roads] illustrated by the exceptional illustrator Ulises Wensell, initially developed by Editorial Santiago Rodríguez in Spain and finally published by Addison-Wesley in the United States, and partially by McGraw-Hill in Mexico, followed the basic principle that guided the Peruvian series *Edad de Oro*: let each page be something children will want to read and re-read. The teacher materials followed the Creative Reading process promoting an empowering dialogue leading to supporting social justice and equality.
The program was enhanced when the

abundant poems were put to music by the gifted composer and singer Suni Paz. Later these poems turned into song have been incorporated into the *Música amiga* program listed at the end of the book in the section of Selective Titles of my work.

Creative Dialoging and Research

When many of my doctoral students at the University of San Francisco selected Participatory Research as the research method for their dissertation, they realized the usefulness of the Creative Dialogue in the process of conducting their dialogue sessions with their participants.

They pointed out the basic coincidence with Paulo Freire's process of reflection and action while acknowledging that the Personal Interpretive Phase present in Creative Reading was particularly useful in the process of dialoguing with their participants.

Once again, the different aspects on my process of learning to be an educator came together.

3. The Power of Children's Books

Learning with Migrant-Farm Working Parents in Pájaro Valley

A young mother, somewhat intimidated in front of a group of nearly a hundred people, is about to read a story written by her daughter. She hesitates, unsure whether the story is appropriate, and apologizes because it contains words which she considers unseemly" with these words I began sharing in the experiences of working with migrant farm-working parents in a chapter titled The Pájaro Valley Experience in Tove Skutnabb Kangas and Jim Cummins seminal book **Minority Education: From Shame to Struggle** (1988).

The meeting where the young mother was sharing her daughter's story was part of a series of monthly evening gatherings of migrant farm-working parents. The objective was to dialogue about their home and school education utilizing children's books as prompts. The chapter from which I quote offers a full description of the program and how to implement similar ones.

Upon welcoming the parents warmly, recognizing the value of their effort to attend a late evening meeting, after having worked all day in the fields, I made a brief introduction to two or three children's books.

Most of the parents had had very little opportunities to receive formal schooling and many of them were illiterate, thus the reason to select picture books of significant content.

The parents were to choose one of the books, which they would later take home, and we encouraged members of the same family to select different books, so that they could have more books to share later with their children. We had observed that not being in the same group fostered more individual participation of both spouses.

The parents gathered in small groups with a teacher facilitator who guided the reading of the book and the ensuing dialogue following the Creative Reading Methodology discussed in the previous chapter.

The facilitators took note on large chart paper of the parents' comments and concluded the small group session by gathering questions and concerns the parents would like to see discussed in the large sessions.

After each small group presented the major topics of their dialogue to the full gathering, parents were invited to read the stories their children and them had written at home in the blank books provided at the end of each session.

After some hesitation, the young mother mentioned at the beginning of this chapter, at last *holds up the title page. It shows a man in field workers' clothing, wearing books and a hat and holding a long whip in his hand. A small girl is standing next to him, reaching barely to his knee. The mother begins to read:* "**I am going to read you a story about a father who returned home from work very angry**", *and here the mother interrupts the story to explain:* "**All of this is true. My husband is much older than me, and he comes home from work very tired. And if the children are talking loudly or making noise, he gets upset and**," *she adds with obvious pain,* "**he sometimes scolds and even punishes them.**"

The audience waited in silence. It seemed as if many could identify with the description, remembering their own tiredness after the long hours of hard work in the fields, some lowered their heads as if acknowledging the mother's pain.

The mother continues reading the story and it is here that the miracle occurs. The story tells us that when the father returned home upset, his daughter asked him what was the matter. Upon finding out that he was tired, she continues: **The old man received a big surprise. His little daughter told him. 'Look, father, I have a cure for your tiredness... I will tell you a very pretty story that Mom read me from a**

book...' and the story was so funny that when the father heard that the pony and the bear had eaten so many apples their bellies were about to burst, he forgot how tired he was, and he laughed and hugged his little daughter and gave her a kiss.

The miracle is that Araceli, the five-year-old girl who dictated this story to her older sister Pati, had discovered the power of books. Not only can they be entertaining and informative, but they offer us possibilities to take action to influence our reality.

Araceli faces frequently a problem: her father gets home so tired from hard labor that he easily becomes upset. But she has learned that she can do something about this problem. And as she ends her story, she addresses her sister Pati, who continues to write down Ceci's words as if they were part of her story: **And haven't you figure out yet, silly, what I am going to do every day when he comes home tired?**
I am going to read him a book.

By her action Araceli not only puts her father in a good mood, but has the satisfaction of knowing that reality can be shaped, influenced and improved upon.

So strong is the impact of this experience that she turns it into a story, and has her sister write it down for her, thus creating a compelling example of what children's interaction with books can produce.

Ceci's story is reproduced in the original Spanish in the chapter from which I quote.

The power of the children's books was revealed not only in the way it affected children, but also their parents.

In the chapter from which I am quoting I include an example of the Creative Dialogue Process using the book *Arturo y Clementina* by Adela Turín.

Arturo and Clementina are turtles. After Clementina shares her dream of being able to paint the beauty she sees, Arturo brings her a painting done by one of his friends and ties it to her shell, as he will later also tie a phonograph when she expresses, she would like to learn to play the flute. Her dream of visiting Italy leads him to add a Murano vase to the multiple things tied to her back which almost prevent her to move... until one day Arturo finds an empty shell and readers are warned that if they see a turtle who travels, and paints, and plays the flute it will probably be Clementina.

Even though the book is part of the series *In favor of girls* the theme of the story allows to generate dialogue about insensitivity to the needs of others, dependence, and lack of communication that are not circumscribed to the dynamic between the sexes. In our experience, while the adults' reflections tended to be about their relationships with their partners, children saw the story as a reflection of relationship between children and parents, who many times prevent children from exploring their talents and abilities.

The discussion with the parents was full of surprises. Instead of feeling intimidated by the subject, it was an excellent catalyst. Many people reported that it was a common experience for them to feel unappreciated by the people around them. And they were able to share their feelings of frustration and fear which resulted when others did not believe in their potential.

*One mother commented that she often feels like Clementina. Although her husband is a very good man, he did not believe in her ability to study and to lean English. "Nonetheless," she said. "I am not remaining silent like Clementina did, but instead make him see that I **can** do things."*

One of the men present quickly made a parallel with his own attitude as a husband, recognizing that he habitually leaves all of the responsibility for the children to his wife. "Maybe what was happening to Clementina was that she was carrying too much weight..." he said, "this makes me think that maybe my wife needs more of my help, and, most of all, that I listen to what her problems are..."

When several years after the initial implementation of the program my daughter, Rosalma Zubizarreta Ada, was invited to develop a manual so that other districts could implement similar projects, I accompanied her to Pájaro Valley and met with some of the parents who years before had attended our meetings.

One of the mothers who had participated in the program proudly invited us to visit the Day Care center for young children she had established with her two daughters, who had both studied Early Childhood Education.

There, in the center of the main room on a tall and narrow table, was displayed a much read copy of **Arturo y Clementina** 'After that story', the mother told us, 'I knew I could create a future for my daughters and me beyond crawling on the earth to pick strawberries... '

Yes, children's books can be very powerful, and an excellent vehicle to facilitate dialogue.

The sessions at Pájaro Valley were a model of honest and courageous sharing, and I will always be grateful to the parents who engaged in critical analysis with me and who shared the books they and their children had written.

The sessions were all videotapes. These tapes, as well as others from similar projects, and numerous examples of books produced by children and parents, are held at the Reinberger Children's Library Center, School of Information, Kent State University, in Ohio, where materials produced by Isabel Campoy and myself or related to our work are archived.

There have been many programs inspired by this work including the program *Libros y Familias* created in Oregon by one of my advisees Dr. Richard Keis. The program is described in his dissertation. And copies of the materials developed in it are also at the Reinberger Library.

Dr. Karen Kaiser another of the doctoral students that I had the pleasure to advise, studied some of these programs in her own dissertation.

My recognition of the value of potential of children's books led me many times to share a picture book in a graduate class to invite reflection.

The Expedition, Willi Baum's wordless book, shows with strikingly bold illustrations a group of European soldiers in full regalia arriving on a steam ship at what looks like a deserted tropical island. On the top of a hill, at the center of the island, shines a white stone temple.

The men leave their ship and follow the captain cutting through the jungle to arrive to the top of the hill where they dissemble the temple pieces, which they carefully carry back to their ship.

There they will find out that the ship's smoke stacks have disappeared. Surprised they look back towards the hill whether the shining white temple has been replaced by colorful smoke stacks.

While the last image showing the men trying to move their ship by rowing brings out initially a moment of laughter, the book provides for the possibility of very deep reflection about the harm of colonization and misappropriation of indigenous rights, making it clear that useless smoke stacks, that will have a negative impact on the environment, have been obtained at the expense of significant cultural art.

I also shared many times Lee Bennet Hopkins poignant memoir in verse *Been to Yesterday* winner of the Christopher Award medal.

This extraordinary book served the dual purpose of reminding educators of the difficult circumstances ignored by us that children may be living through and also to introduce the idea of journal writing in many of my courses. It was always received very warmly by my doctoral students.

4. The World is a Classroom

At a moment in my life when I craved solicitude and silence, I was faced with having to go to a Conference at Las Vegas. My initial reaction was of concern, Las Vegas seemed very remote from peace and silence.

My teaching assistant at the time, Constance Beutel, hearing of this concern, replied very firmly: "Make Las Vegas an ashram." From anyone else I would have thought this a silly joke, but I had learned to listen and appreciate Connie's recommendations. So, I travelled to Las Vegas determined to make it an ashram. And thus, every time I crossed the hotel casino to get to my room, I ignored the coin machines, the noise and the smoke, and focused on the individuals sitting in front of each machine.

I let my heart fill with love, without trying to imagine what had brought them to that place —loneliness, hope, boredom, expectations— I focused on thinking of the human being they were, the baby they had been, the joy their presence had given others, the beauty in their souls, perhaps hidden and ignored by others, perhaps invisible to themselves.

Las Vegas was indeed an ashram once I knew what to seek.

And Connie's metaphor remained with me and I am using it now when I state that the World is a classroom, when we realize that all our actions have the potency of being a lesson, we either teach or learn.

I am grateful to the numerous teachers that have participated in presentations and workshop offered during conferences or at their districts or schools. Listening to their questions and their experiences was a constant education on the art of teaching.

My gratitude is equally profound to the hundreds of parents, particularly migrant farm-working parents and other Latina/Latino parents who have been open to share with me their dreams and concerns regarding the future of their children. They have been a reason to renew constantly my commitment towards creating a just society and a source of hope.

As they were willing to share their own experiences of immigration and hard-work, my conviction of recognizing each individual as the protagonist of her/his own life was reaffirmed, as was the need to continue promoting that everyone see themselves as authors of their own life and be willing to write or tell their life story.

The process promotes authorship of teachers so that they can become models of authorship to their students. It promotes authorship of parents so that they can stand at a level of equality with the teachers, both authors of their own lives. This process, which I had carried on in many sites, principally in California and Texas, became much more formalized when Aurora Martínez, editor at Allyn & Bacon, while attending one of our sessions, seeing the enthusiastic response of the audience, invited us to create the book *Authors in the Classroom: A Transformative Education Process.* My generous daughter, Rosalma Zubizarreta-Ada, collaborated with us adding to the book an important component on anti-bias education.

The awakening of self, facilitated by *Authors in the classroom* as a transformative process to promote authorship in teachers and students and the students' parents met with the same type of enthusiasm in the most diverse environment.

In rural schools in México as well as in New York City, in Madrid as well as in the Czech Republic, in Guam as well as in Italy, in Bulgaria and Puerto Rico, Hungary or Stockton, Dallas or Fresno, Isabel and I found that everyone was grateful to be invited to look deeply inside and discover the metaphors that describe their being or the simple but powerful words who celebrate the heroes in their lives.

That educators who embraced this process come decades later to reminiscence with us the power of their own story or decide to extend this possibility to hundreds of children, as Estela Olivera who was our student one summer in Madrid, has been doing through the LA Best after school program, simply confirm the power of language when it is used for self-discovery.

My gratitude to all the teachers, parents, students, administrators and librarians, who by having the courage to speak the truth have acknowledged their role as authors of the most valuable story, the one reflecting who they are.

More information on how to facilitate authorship and examples of authentic books written by teachers, parents and students can be found at:

www.authorsintheclassroom.com

5. Learning to Listen Loudly

While talking about the importance of listening, whether to students or to research participants, I used to insist on the need to hear not just what it is said, but also how and when it is said, and furthermore, to listen to what is not said.

At some point one of the doctoral students responded to my recommendations saying: "What you want us to do is **to listen loudly!**" Her pun was successful and "the need of listening loudly" was frequently mentioned in my classes.

I don't have a recollection of when it became apparent to me that the quality of our listening is a most significant aspect of our task as educators, but there are three moments that have remained forever present for me. Here are the stories:

The first bilingual program in Detroit before the passing of the state law, was a federally funded Title VII program. Knowing my efforts in support of the passing of the bilingual law I was invited to visit this program.

After visiting one of the classrooms, the teacher shared her concern about a child which remained very passive and silent all the time. She had tried to gain his interest in books but he seemed uninterested on any topic she suggested.

I sat with the child determined to discover something that would interest him. An experience I had while a High School teacher, which I will narrate later, had convinced me that every child has an interest, albeit sometimes an unexpected one.

Since general questions like "What is something you would like to read about?" "Or what do you like to do?" had given no results, since the child limited himself to look at me silently, I began to mention planes, trains, cars, trucks, motorcycles, bicycles. But no kind of vehicle seemed to interest him, nor did football, baseball, basketball or sports of any kind. Whales, dolphins, sharks or living being in the ocean also failed to awaken his interest which was not moved either by cats, dogs, or horses.

Giving up easily is not part of my nature and I strongly believed in the importance of establishing a connection with the child, and I continued trying. When "Is there something you would like to know about, that perhaps we can find about together?" did not get a response, I changed the question to: "Is there something you know about that I probably don't know and you can tell me?"

Yes, indeed, there was. The child was an expert of all things to do with pigeons. His father, the janitor of a tall Detroit building, had been given access to the roof top and had built there several pigeon coops to raise pigeons of different breeds. And how much it is there to learn about pigeons if you had the interest, patience and opportunity that child had!

He was a true expert in breeding, raising, and enjoying the rich diversity of pigeons. The only problem is that the life of pigeons is not a typical curriculum item.

My experience in Perú, a few years before, had been similar although perhaps more dramatic for me because in that case I was the teacher during three High School subjects for two students I could not reach.

It was my first year of teaching at the *Abraham Lincoln Bilingual School* in Lima. I had been contracted to teach the High School Language and Literature Courses. Then, without previous notice, two Senior courses were assigned to my original teaching load, one   Philosophy and the other Psychology.

Two of the students in the Senior class were twins, quiet and respectful, they did not participate in class discussions, and, when I received their first written assignments, I discovered with dismay that the papers were basically unreadable.

I returned to them the papers covered with my corrections only to receive from there onwards their assignments beautifully typed and very correctly written. It was obvious to me they were not the authors of such papers and demanded that they continue to turn in their assignments handwritten.

This led to a call for order by a senior faculty, the president of the teacher's association. He explained to me I was making a grave mistake in demanding work from these students. Had I failed to notice that this private school was owned by the parents? Did I not know that the father of the twins was the major stock holder?

While I tried to explain that I was dismayed that these boys had been allowed to reach the last year of High School unable to write, he assured me that, unless I changed my attitude, I should know I would not be rehired the following year.

Firmly warned, I returned to my classes, but I could not accept to ignore the situation and not try to do something for these boys.

A long-time secretary of the school gave me a little insight of what she considered to have been the beginning of the problem.

Ever since Kindergarten the set of blond twins with blue eyes and rosy cheeks, seemed particularly adorable in Perú, where most children have a darker complexion. Since they were quiet and gentle, they had awakened tenderness on teachers and since they seemed to be always content being by themselves, why bother them with tedious tasks? The boys learned to read, but did show interest in writing, so they were never expected to do much. And, their grades were excellent since their father was such a gentleman and major supporter of the school.

Her explanation shared some light but did not excuse the teachers' behaviors. I set out to try to find something that could interest these young men. The rest of the students were reading World, Latin American and Peruvian literature. I had made efforts to draw the interest of those who were less motivated readers with books that could be within their reach: Mark Twain, Charles Dickens, Alexander Dumas, Jules Verne, Salgari, proved to be good stepping stones for those who had not done much reading before, and now were becoming enthusiastic readers, and were beginning to enjoy more serious literature. But the twins did not seem to care about any of these books.

I stayed with them during recess trying to give them some basic writing lessons hoping that if we could find topics of their interest the lessons would be less painful... all to no avail. Until one day...

It was recess time and for once I had not retained them for a lesson. Nevertheless, they stayed in the classroom. I went out for a moment and, when I came back, I could not believe my eyes.

They were both absorbed in a huge book and animatedly talking to each other...

they, whose voice tended not to be much more than a murmur

What was that book? I approached them and asked them in as natural a voice as I could master, what were they reading. They proudly showed me a very thick catalogue of machinery for the production of bread.

Their father was the owner of a major bakery and they were considering making a total change of equipment. And for once in their life there was a disagreement between the twins since each favored a different kind of process and equipment.

What a joy! There was something that could move these kids: not cars, sports, music, games, animals, adventures, like the rest of the class, but BREAD!

From then on bread became a necessary topic in each of our classes: whether Philosophy, Psychology or Literature no class failed to give bread (literally or metaphorically) a major place.

On those prehistoric times before Internet this implied many hours of going through books to find the appropriate readings or examples that mentioned bread, wheat, flour, the making of flour, the raising of the dough, the metaphoric references to bread as sustenance... and great efforts to find ways to weave all that unto the curriculum.

On one course, each of the twins were asked to give an individual presentation of his favorite form of making bread, and at another course they were invited to debate with each other on the benefit of the process and equipment each favored.

Every student was amazed that after having been together in class with the twins for many years they were hearing them for the first time speak loud and clear and showing an almost passionate interest on a topic.

Personally, I promised myself I would never cease to look for the one interest hidden in each student. And since bread has such a prevailing presence —and I so delight on good bread—this story has remained very alive and present for me.

The third and last story I will mention is of a somewhat different nature and took place, many years ago, in New York City, in a school at a neighborhood so deprived I had to argue with the taxi driver to take me there.

I had been invited to share a story with children, and, to my great surprise I found myself in an assembly room. The second-grade children from a couple of classes, for whom I was to story tell, had been placed in a large circle and behind them there was an even larger circle of teachers and aides that have been invited to see a demonstration.

Contrary to what most people think, I am a very timid person, who struggles to overcome my shyness when doing so may be of benefit to others. So, after a moment of hesitation, I began to tell the folk story of the hen who loved to saw and always carried scissors, needle and threat in her apron's pocket.

Half way through the story, although the children were listening attentively, I began to have misgivings: *Why was I telling these children a story of something so remote to themselves? Had any of these children ever seen a hen? Why was I taking them to the middle of a wood, when they lived in a jungle of buildings with boarded windows?* But, of course, the children were expecting the continuation of the story and I went on.

When I finished, I began engaging them in the Creative Reading dialogue. The children were very much opened to sharing. When I asked how was the hen feeling inside the sack carried by the wolf, I got a variety of expected answers, like "worried" or "afraid". One particular child eagerly said: "I know, I know, she felt just like my friend did when she got trapped in the elevator".

At that moment I knew that while we definitely need diverse books that present the diversity of human reality, something I have always promoted, the relevance of a story does not depend always on its setting but on its message.

The little Puerto Rican child in New York, which probably had never seen a wood, a chicken or a wolf, knew about the fear of being trapped in a place one does not want to be.

Relieved seeing that the story had been meaningful to them, I kept looking at the children, to continue engaging as many as possible in the sharing. Across the large circle I observed a child whose face let me know she had experienced a strong feeling. So, I walked over to her and asked: "How do you think the hen was feeling?" She raised her eyes to me and said sadly "Very lonely."

"Very lonely" was a surprising answer. The other children had said "upset" "angry", "worried" and "scared" and even given one example of a personal experience of being scared, but "very lonely"?

I then lowered myself to the level of her little chair and looking at her, asked her very softly, "Do you ever feel lonely?"

"Every day" was her answer. "When?" I asked back, in the same soft voice. "Every day," she answered, "when I get home."

Observing the key hanging from her neck, I nodded and she went on: "And, now, since the baby was born, I feel even more lonely, because Mom has to go and pick up the baby before coming home, so I have to wait longer for her..." And then she paused and said: "And I worry the baby must also be lonely in a strange house."

All I could do was smile at her, letting her know I fully understood her. And added, softly, just for her, "I hear how lonely you feel. You are very brave and kind. The baby is fortunate to have you as a sister."

The children were dismissed and the administrator who had organized the event wanted to hear from the teachers. One of them stood up and said: "This is the first time in all these months that we hear the voice of that last child who spoke. We have already sent a request for a speech evaluation. We thought she could not talk."

That day I received one of the most significant lessons about teaching. The pain that child was suffering was such, that unless she could voice it, no other word would find its way out of her voice.

Listening loudly, yes, even listening to the face of a child who needs to speak, but needs to have the opportunity to say what's in her heart.

6. Teaching at the University of San Francisco

The winter of 1976 was one of the coldest registered until that time in Chicago. The cold winds from the North made us feel we had reached the Artic, especially when my eyelashes froze from walking from our front door to the car.

Precisely as I was questioning what could possibly justify for a Caribbean woman to live and raise her family in such inclement weather, I attended a conference in the Bay Area. And, while it may sound very trite, I became one of those who have left their heart in San Francisco.

Having made the decision to move West I felt very grateful to have three job offers. One was from the University of Colorado, bringing back cherished memories of Loretto Heights College; the other was from the University of Arizona in Tucson. At that time the state had a strong bilingual program, and I had become familiar with the city numerous presentations there, and not only I had friends in the city but I admired the faculty at the School of Education. The third offer came from San Diego State University.

The choice was very difficult to make. The University of Colorado and the University of Arizona were stronger universities, with doctoral programs, but in San Diego, although I had only been there once, I had wonderful activist friends, both at San Diego State and at the school district, and the idea of joining them in a strong community action was very appealing to me.

Everyone I had spoken to about my newly found love for San Francisco had discouraged me about the possibility of finding a university position there: it seemed as if everyone wanted to be in the San Francisco Bay Area and finding a position there would be next to impossible, so I had put it out of my mind, and was leaning towards accepting the position at San Diego State, although I was postponing the difficult choice to the maximum possible.

When I attended the Conference of the National Association for Bilingual Education (NABE) being held that year in Texas, the need to make a decision was foremost in my mind. Would I choose mountains, desert or, ocean? Which would be a better environment for my children's future? Where would they be happier? Because one thing was very clear in my mind, having lived in three countries and seven states I was definitely hoping that this would be the last move, at least for some time.

At the NABE Conference I was giving an all- day pre-conference workshop on the Teaching of Reading and Spanish Language Arts. I was filled with enthusiasm to meet a large room full of eager teachers and their interest and participation were fulfilling, all I could have expected... but something bothered me.

At the back of the room there was a gentleman I had never met before. Dressed on a three-pieces suit he did not fit my image of a classroom teacher. I was used to have administrators attend my presentations, but usually not an all-day workshop, and certainly not taking down every word I spoke. At the lunch time break, while many of the teachers approached me, he simply vanished. I thought I had seen the last of him, and forgot about him, while listening to the teachers and enjoying the conversation of a few of them with whom I shared lunch.

But when I returned to the meeting room for the afternoon session, the gentleman was sitting quietly in the back of the room. When the session finished, I was again surrounded by the teachers who had questions, or comments, or wanted to take a photo... The mysterious elegant man waited until all participants had left and, then, approached me.

"Would you like to have a glass of wine?" the question did surprise me, but I quickly answered, "Yes, I would!" although I did not add the rest that was in my mind "now, I will finally know who you are."

We walked to the bar of the hotel where the conference was being held, and after he ordered the wine, with no preamble, he simply asked: "Would you like a position at the University of San Francisco?" And, then with a smile, he added, "You have already passed the interview."

José Llanes would become a friend forever, and while I always be grateful for fulfilling what I thought was an impossible dream, living and teaching in San Francisco, the friendship grew as I got to know José and admire his intelligence, his character, his values, the extraordinary person he is.

The program Dr. José Llanes had invited me to join was a new graduate program in Multicultural Education at the University of San Francisco (USF). He had initiated the program with the support of Dean Allen Calvin and a Title VII grant from the US

Department of Education for developing educators who would in their own turn, mentor and support bilingual teachers.

During the first year the program had offered Bilingual Education Credentials and Masters in four language specialties: Spanish, Chinese, Japanese and Filipino. Now the Multicultural Program would be expanded with a Doctoral Program.

While I had begun my formal university career in the United States as a professor of Latin American Literature at Emory University, I had become very active in the bilingual education movement during the three years I spent teaching at Mercy College in Detroit, presently Mercy University. In addition to establishing the first bilingual teacher training program in Michigan, I had helped to organize the Michigan Association for Bilingual Education, of which I was the first Vice-President, and had planned and hosted at Mercy College the first Michigan state conference on Latino Education which we called *Michigan Education and the Latino.*

As a member of the National Association of Bilingual Education (NABE), I founded the *NABE Journal* and was its first Editor-in-Chief.

While literature was still a passion for me, I felt a strong calling to the work of developing educators. I wanted to help grow leaders who, in addition to understanding the significance of bilingualism, would also be deeply informed by the perspectives of multiculturalism and critical pedagogy. I accepted Dr. Llanes' offer with pleasure and enthusiasm.

José Llanes' inspiring vision was to create a program where all involved, 20 doctoral students, all Title VII grant recipients, and 7 faculty members, some of whom were also working on their doctoral degree, would engage in intensive seminars every week-end for a whole academic year. To this end, he invited the most distinguished scholars in Bilingual Education at the time, including Professors Joshua Fishman, Bruce Gaardner, Wallace Lambert, Eduardo Hernández-Chávez, and Henry

Trueba, to spend one or two week-ends at USF discussing their work with the doctoral students and professors.

It was both an exhilarating and exhausting first year. All of our doctoral students had full-time employment in addition to the weekend seminars, while all of our professors had a full schedule of Masters and Credential courses that we taught during the week. The intensive seminars ran from early Saturday morning through Sunday evening every weekend. While it was a challenge to keep up with the readings, everyone was delighted with the opportunity to work so closely with such inspiring scholars.

As a result of the intense pace, students were able to complete all 60 units of their doctoral courses by the end of the year, with the only remaining requirement being the completion of their dissertation. This proved to be very difficult. Since the students were no longer attending class, they were facing the task of writing a dissertation on their own, a process that most found daunting. Remember these were pre-Internet times.

At the end of that first year, Dr. Llanes left the University of San Francisco for a position at another university, and I was asked by Dean Allen Calvin to take responsibility for the doctoral program. Thus, began the on-going work of re-designing the program based on what we had learned that first year.

Over the next several years, many changes were made to the structure of the program while seeking to preserve its original spirit of high-level inquiry, collegiality, and commitment to excellence. Classes were still taking place on weekends to accommodate working professionals, yet they were scheduled every other weekend and included Friday evening and all-day Saturday, but not Sunday.

The course work was redesigned to include courses that would assist students in thinking about and planning for their dissertation from the beginning of the program. In combination with the slower pace, this meant that the course work now stretched out over three or four years, rather than be completed in only one. On the other hand, this enabled students to finish their dissertations shortly after completing the courses, or in some cases even concurrently.

During my time at USF, there were significant changes in the administration, which resulted in varying levels of support for our program, whose name changed to International Multicultural Education [IME]. Over the years, my own role has been primarily as Professor and Title VII coordinator, which included writing the funding proposal to Washington, only once I held an administrative role, something I had no real interest in doing. Yet, during periods of difficulty and challenge, I found that by working together with the students, they were the ones who were able to maintain the integrity of the program.

Throughout my years as a professor, my guiding principle was the search for a creative balance between idealism and practicality, the don Quixote and Sancho combination in me. On the one hand, I felt a strong commitment to creating a classroom community conducive to personal transformation, where students can grow intellectually and affectively, where they can reflect deeply and critically on their own experiences and on the experiences of others. Several of the practices I have developed for this purpose will be described more fully below.

At the same time, I developed an equally strong commitment to helping students master the practical requirements for obtaining a degree, so that they were able to apply what they had learned in ever-widening spheres of professional influence. I feel a great sense of accomplishment knowing that many of my former students have become administrators, principals, program coordinator, assistant superintendents and superintendents working to create better educational opportunities for many, in turn, several have become college professors throughout California and beyond, and in that capacity as well they have continued to support the growth and development of others.

On the process of finding more efficient ways of facilitating that students would complete their dissertations and obtain the degree in a timely fashion, avoiding ending with the condition of ABD (all but dissertation), the condition of many of the applicants to the program I found inspiration in Gabriela Pisano, the first student to graduate from the program, in only three years.

Gabriela's motivation and determination became manifested in our initial meeting. When in answer to her question of how long it would take to complete the degree, I told her that current students were taking four and even five years, she asked me directly: "What would be the minimum time and what would it take to achieve it?"

After she explained her goal of being the youngest Latina Dean in a Community College, our informative session turned into an advisement session. She left my office determined to achieve her goals in three years.

I never believed that graduating quickly should be the ultimate goal and certainly that it should not be achieved by sacrificing the quality of the experience, yet, at the same time, Gabriela made it very clear that for students a timely graduation could hold great professional value.

Establishing processes that would assist students in timely graduation had a great significance in the development of the program. A significant proportion of our students were being supported by Title VII Fellowships. The fact that our students graduated, with significant dissertations, at the end of their three years fellowship or shortly after, contributed to the renewal of the funding and the increase in the numbers of new fellows based on our excellent track record of graduation. Thus, our students' efforts to graduate timely were beneficial not only to them but to others coming behind them.

Graduates from the IME Program are frequent speakers at the annual conference of the California Association for Bilingual Education [CABE] and have hold diverse positions within that organization, while one of my former advisees and Title VII Fellow, Dr. Santiago Wood is the director of the National Association for Bilingual Education [NABE].

And the silent presence of that elegant gentleman who took notes of all my words at a NABE pre-conference workshop in what turned out to be an unsuspected interview will remain always a most significant and cherished moment in my memory.

7. The Practice of Freedom

Freedom is a highly acclaimed concept. Wars, horrible and destructive as is the nature of wars, have been fought to defend this principle. Songs and poems have been created to celebrate this valuable human right. Yet, not sufficient attention is paid to realize the exact nature of freedom, the fallacy in declaring oneself, or anyone, free.

Freedom is not a permanent state that once achieved remains constant. Freedom is a momentary experience that must be manifested in each action. And achieving freedom is far from a simple process.

Much of the time when we believe to be acting freely, we are, instead, acting out of inertia or habit, imitating others, or following, unconsciously, what we have been taught or the designs of someone else.

A moment of reflection will allow us to see how we tend to do things the way we have always done or the way we have seen our parents or elders do it, the way it is common in our community, the "way things are done".

We have been instilled principles like "this is the way things are" or "if it is not broken do not fix it" which assumes that only things broken need improvement.

It's inspiring that human beings are willing to challenge the limits imposed by physical reality. While we are not born with wings, we have found the ways to fly and even travel in space; while we are not born with gills, we have ways of breathing under water and exploring the depths of the ocean. We have equally refused to be limited by our normal eyesight and have created microscopes, telescopes, x-ray machines and continue to develop much more complex instruments to reach what eyes cannot reach.

Yet, in contrast to that determination to not accept limits imposed by physical realities, humanity has not challenged the social conditions to the extent of eliminating poverty, inequality and violence, and achieving peace.

Nor have humanity accepts its full responsibility to maintain the health of the environment it inhabits and protect all life forms, challenging the harms that colonialism and unbridle capitalism create for most, if not all, human beings.

Changing the way things have always been, to achieve what things should be, we must free ourselves from the belief that social change is not possible and reclaim our freedom and put it at the service of the change we want to bring about.

To act freely requires three very specific stages. While the descriptions offered here are very simple, they refer to complex processes not necessarily easy to follow.

First, we must know what are the alternatives to any action or decision we are about to take.

As long as we are alive there are always alternatives to each action or thought.

Second, we must reflect on what are the conceivable consequences, moral and practical outcomes, of each alternative.

What repercussions will our decision have for us and others in the present and future? Only when the consequences have been honestly analyzed will be ready to act in freedom.

Third, we must have the courage to choose the alternative that is in accord with our own principles.

Only then can we consider our action a free action. But we must remain aware that this process must be repeated every time.

We must also remember that inaction is also an action, that witnessing wrong and not stop, prevent or modify it, is also an action.

We are responsible both for what we do and what we fail to do. And inaction may be also a result of not having learned to act freely.

For me, teaching the essence of freedom is a basic principle of an education conducive to conscientious and responsible societies.

8. The Challenge of Research:
Facing Our Fears as a Practice of Empowerment

After Dr. Llanes' departure, one of the first things I began to realize was how much support our students would need in order to complete their dissertations. While most of our doctoral students had been able of completing their course requirements, even in the most difficult circumstances, very few came already knowing how to do independent research.

During my 29 years at USF, over 300 dissertations were completed in the IME Program. I have had the pleasure of personally chairing 157 of them, and also be the second or third reader for numerous others. Many of these students writing these dissertations had not previously written a substantial Master's thesis. A considerable number of them had been educated abroad or did not have English as their first language, and almost all of them were working full time while attending the doctoral program. Given these conditions, what we were able to accomplish would not have been possible, without a coherent pedagogical philosophy and practice based on both transformation and empowerment. In order to help my doctoral students with their theses, I had to draw on an important lesson I had learned earlier in life, about the need to face our fears.

I still remember vividly my first encounter with this insight, many years before I came to teach at USF. At the time, I was living in Lima, attending the Pontificia Universidad Católica del Perú while working full-time as a high-school teacher. I applied for a position to teach high school Spanish Language Arts and Literature at the Colegio Abraham Lincoln. After I obtained the position my load was considerably increased when I was asked to teach the courses on Psychology, Philosophy and Logic, courses in which I had limited preparation since they were not my major.

And I was struggling to stay one lesson ahead of my students.

One morning while writing at the blackboard, our most common teaching tool at the time, I noticed that I was attempting to disguise my handwriting to cover my uncertainty about the spelling of a word I needed to write. Since spelling was still troublesome for me, I had developed a calligraphy where **c, s,** and **z** were indistinguishable as were **b** and **v.**

At that moment of reckoning, I also realized that I had developed the art of giving ambiguous answers, delving into another subject in which I had some expertise, or else telling distracting stories whenever I was unsure of the answer to the students' questions. Having by then lived, besides my native Cuba, in three states of the United States, and in Spain, gave me ample materials that fascinated my Peruvian students, most of whom had never been outside of Perú.

Chalk in hand, I stood frozen in front of the blackboard, with my back to the students, while question followed question in my mind. *What was I really trying to achieve? I asked myself. What value did all my dissembling had for my students? How could I possibly believe that I was gaining their respect? And if they did indeed hold me in some respect, what false model were they respecting? Was I really teaching them to cheat, to be insincere, to hide their limitations rather than confront them?*

I can still see the shock in my student's faces when I dropped the chalk and turned to them to share my thoughts. After owning up to my difficulties with spelling, I asked if any of them also experienced a similar challenge. When several hands went up, I suggested that we could all work together on mastering spelling, and that I would welcome the opportunity to learn alongside them. For those who did not have difficulties with spelling, the vocabulary enrichment aspect of the exercises that I decided to create would make it worth their time.

From then on, we opened every class with a few minutes spelling and vocabulary exercise. A few years later, the collected set of exercises I devised for this purpose became my first published book: *Ortografía Práctica* (Ada de Zubizarreta, 1964).

My newly-found commitment to recognizing my limitations was not restricted to spelling. I committed myself to attempt to answer honestly every question that my students asked in the classroom, even if the answer had to be, "I don't know enough to say, but I will research your question." In that pre-Internet times, the search would many times require to spend quite a bit of time in the library. Soon I realized that the learning would be more fruitful if, instead of expecting me to find the answer, I invited the students to search alongside me. And often that search for answers inspired group or class projects.

Creating this kind of learning climate with my doctoral students many years later was a more challenging endeavor. They, too, had learned many coping mechanisms to disguise their own weaknesses. Yet, the most difficult task that they would be facing was writing their dissertation, and I decided early on that it would be helpful for all of us to face this hurdle and its attendant fears head first.

It was a liberating process to work together to analyze our own fears of research. From the perspective of critical pedagogy, we can see that keeping these fears alive, benefits only those who seek to control the gates of power. Complex nomenclature can easily intimidate us, yet learning the language of research is an important and necessary step toward empowering ourselves.

At the same time, I found it helpful to begin with validating what we already know. An encouraging first step is to realize that we have been informal researchers all of our lives, with our own life-long inquiries and our own history of conjecturing and testing and experimentation, that has given rise to all of the valuable learning and discoveries that we have made along the way. By deepening this experiential understanding of ourselves as researchers, we become much better positioned for learning the various protocols of formal research methods.

Patricia Maguire (1987, p. 17) in her seminal book **Doing Participatory Research: a feminist perspective** pointed out very clearly the need to recognize the existence of a dominant research paradigm. "…many people don't know their research practices reflect a world view at all, so they cannot consciously question underlying assumptions or actively consider alternatives.

Constance M. Beutel, my generous teaching assistant at the time suggested that we would write a manual that would compile not only what we were learning about Participatory Research from the most significant authors writing on this topic, but also from the research the doctoral students have been doing. This handbook **Participatory Research as a Dialogue for Social Action** (Ada and Beutel, 1993), although never formally published became a valuable resource for numerous students who continued to expand the reflection on the potential of Participatory Research to bring about transformation in a multiplicity of settings. The list of dissertation titles can give an idea od the diverse applications of this methodology.

Another key aspect of demystifying the dissertation process is to break the process down into component parts. Rather than focusing on the 100-plus pages of the final voluminous product, students can learn to analyze a thesis as a document composed of distinct sections. With some advanced planning, many of those sections can be developed independently, as part of the course work for their doctoral courses. By designing the process in this manner, many students were able to complete their dissertations within a relatively short time after finishing their course work.

As an author I am frequently approached by people who tell me of their desire to author a book and who try to explain the reasons they have not done so. Many times, I find myself telling, as I tell the teachers I encourage to create their own books, in a very firm voice that "no one has ever written a book". When they look at me trying to find an explanation to my statement, I clarify that no one has ever written a book as complete task, but rather we write a sentence that turns into a paragraph, that becomes a page that added to others forms one of the chapters of what will eventually become a book.

This same kind of reassurance was important for my students to whom I also told that just as human beings we become what we eat, what we say, what we think, what we do, as writers we tend to write like the books we read. When facing with the task of writing a dissertation it is a good practice to look through many dissertations and then to read those that appeal the most to us. They will most likely influence how we write our own.

These, then, are some of the steps that I discovered in the process of helping students learn the discipline of research. It took me a few years to overcome the anxieties instilled by my own educational experiences, but when I was finally able to give the title *The Joy of Research*, to the advisement handbook we prepared for the doctoral students, I knew we were embarked on a truly empowering adventure.

9.Creating a Broad-based Community of Learners

Over the years, I have noticed that my best courses, the ones in which students have been most engaged, have usually been the ones that included students with varying levels of program experience. Newer students clearly benefited from the example and participation of more experienced students, who were already accustomed to the highly interactive approach of our program. At the same time, experienced students would often comment on how their own understanding deepened whenever they had the opportunity to explain something to a newer student, who also many times came out with questions from different perspectives.

There were two related factors in our program design that allowed this kind of rich interaction to take place, and I worked hard to protect these design elements. While many programs benefit from having a cohort structure in which students follow an established sequence of courses, I believe our program benefited from the decision to do things differently.

Out of five different programs in the USF School of Education, the International Multicultural Program was the only one that did not have a cohort structure with an established sequence of courses. One of the initial reasons for not choosing a cohort structure was that we did not want to force students to all take the same courses. As our students came from such diverse backgrounds, it seemed important to offer them some choices that recognized their previous knowledge and diverse experiences. In turn, offering students more alternatives meant that as professors, we were less likely to have students in our courses who had not freely chosen to be there. For me this was of paramount importance.

While I was never able to convince the administration to do away with all course prerequisites, I was often able to find creative alternatives. For example, I sometimes recommended that students take the Advanced Research Course twice: once when they first entered the program, to get a closer look at the end result of the process upon which they were embarking, and then, again, when they were further along. However, as students cannot receive credit for the same course twice, allowing them to sign up during their first or second semester for a directed study that was fulfilled by attending the Advanced Research Course, which they would attend again as registered students in the curse a few semesters later, was sometimes a workable way of meeting both the University requirements and their educational needs.

It's my experience that it is important for students to develop an on-going sense of connection with one another. While we chose to not have a formal cohort structure, I encouraged students to develop their own "affinity groups" to support one another through the process. These have often been groups of two, three, or four students, frequently at different stages of the program. Having students at different stages of the program attending classes together resulted in the development of a larger learning community that felt more like a family. Continuing students became links between those students who were just graduating and others who were just starting the program.

Over time, at the request of my advisees, I began offering voluntary retreats as way to strengthen this feeling of broader community. Usually our teaching weekends included a Friday evening class followed by a full day of classes on Saturday. Twice a year, during the first teaching weekend of the semester, my advisees and I would be willing to add an extra Saturday evening and the following Sunday and gather at an off-campus retreat site. This allowed the students, who were often traveling to the program from all over California and neighboring states, to meet with one another outside of class, to develop friendships, offer and receive support, delve more deeply on topics of mutual interest, and even design projects together.

The retreat was not directly connected with the University. While everyone was invited, attendance was voluntary. There was no charge for attending, although every person, including me, paid for their own lodging and meals. As a group, we would create an agenda together, offering both small group and large group sessions so that everyone would have the opportunity to explore their particular concerns.

Students valued the retreats so highly that many graduates would continue to attend. These graduates would work with one another on writing journal articles, on preparations for promotion and tenure, and on social issues of common interest. In addition, many offered themselves as mentors for newly enrolled students. Frequently they brought with them friends they were encouraging to apply to the program. On this way many students' first acquaintance with the program took place during the retreats that they attended as prospective students.

These practices led to bring into the program many like-minded people. The fact that before applying to the program they had a previous idea of the spirit of the group facilitated their engagement and resulted in strengthening our community.

10. Key Pedagogical Models, Principles and Guidelines

As I engaged in sharing the evolution of my pedagogical approach, there are a number of teachers, influences, and experiences that I would like to acknowledge, beginning with my first formal teaching experience which took place while I was still in college.

When I first came to the United States as a young foreign-student I had received a scholarship from Loretto Heights College in Colorado. As a native Spanish-speaker I was expected to assist in the Spanish courses, modeling the oral language. An unexpected event, the fact that the elderly sister who was to be the professor of Spanish 101 and Spanish 201, had a stroke right before the beginning of the Fall semester, led the Dean to ask me to take over the classes for a few days until they could procure a new professor. As the new professor was difficult to obtain, they decided that "the Cuban girl" was doing such a good job that there was no need to hire anyone. And under some supervisor from the other sister who taught the most advanced courses, I was fully in charge to teach not only Spanish 101 and 201, but also, the next semester Spanish 102 and 202.

This probably was only possible because I come from a family of educators. My maternal great-grandparents had a small private school in Madrid. For some years my maternal grandparents had their own very innovative private school in Camagüey, Cuba, the city where I was born. Later, my grandmother created the first night school for working women in the province, while my grandfather had been all along a Professor of French and of Spanish Literature at our Instituto de Segunda Enseñanza, a college preparatory high school, where my father also taught.

Two of my mother's sisters had doctorate degrees in Education, one of them teaching at Havana's Teacher's College, the third was an elementary school teacher. And although my mother would not become formally a teacher until many years later, in the United States, she was a born educator. Probably the most common topics of conversations during meals at my home were about methodology and teaching practices, in particular since for four years we had three young women studying to be teachers boarding with us and my mother would coach them on their demonstrations and student teaching practices.

When I began teaching high school in Perú I developed an interest in the theories behind what so far had been for me an art and a practice. My experiences with my high-school students, some of which I have described earlier in this essay, led me to search, in Lima's used-books stores, the only available to my meager economy, for further inspiration.

Some of my most memorable finds included a book by a teacher in an Argentinian rural school, identified only as Maestro Romualdo, who had published the writings of his students.

Very inspiring also was a series of books by Celestine Freinet (1986/1969; also 1975/1973 & 1976/1974). Freinet's concept of "the classroom as a publishing house" was a great revelation for me.

These readings led me to encourage my students at the *Abraham Lincoln Bilingual School* to write extensively. We developed a simple mimeographed newspaper they chose to call *El mosquito*. The students were so excited about seeing their writing "published" that they set out to secure advertisement that allowed the development of a small but nicely printed magazine *Lincoln y Nosotros* [Lincoln and Us].

At the time, unhappy with the published text books available to me, I slowly began creating my own classroom materials, which I typed and printed using that prehistoric instrument called a mimeograph. Because I could not imagine myself having to redo the work every year, I put great effort on each lesson, knowing that the next year I could concentrate on developing new ones, and in this way the materials developed by me keep accumulating.

I included students' compositions as models in the mimeographed pages. When those mimeographed pages became books many students' compositions were included. In the two books I published on creative writing, *Ver y describir* [To See and Describe] (1965) and *Oír y narrar* [To Hear and Narrate] (1966) and the high school text books *Castellano I, II* and *III*. The students' writings were analyzed with as much care and literary criticism respect as I did with the models from famous writers also included.

Throughout the years, having been fortunate to reencounter many of my former students, while taking about their experiences in our classes, the word "respect" is constantly repeated. They value and appreciate that they felt so much respected, and the fact that I chose to publish their writing and the treatment their compositions received, is one of the examples they mention of the respect they so much valued.

The most significant finding I made in Lima of written pedagogy was the work of Paulo Freire (1970, 1982, 1997), whose books were banned at the time in many countries of Latin America. Some mimeographed copies that had been smuggled all the way from Chile, where Freire had been living in exile from Brazil, circulated as treasure passing from hand to hand at the courtyard of the Universidad Católica del Perú, where I was studying. When I read Freire's writing, every word rang true. He was giving voice to the stirrings that had been arising from my own experiences in the classroom. What a gift to find such a teacher to guide the rest of my journey! Yet it was the International Multicultural program at USF, where I arrived a decade after first encountering Freire, that offered me the context and opportunity to explore in much greater depth how these ideals might be put into practice, as I continued to learn and grow as a teacher.

At the *Colegio Alexander von Humboldt* we studied the literature of notable Peruvian authors who were denouncing the oppression and injustice suffered by the indigenous population of Peru, both in the countryside and in the *barriadas*, the shanty towns around Lima. The students were very much incensed as they became aware that what they read in the writings of Ciro Alegría, José María Arguedas, Enrique Congrains, José Ramón Ribeyro and Sebastián Salazar Bondy, were depictions of a cruel reality.

It seemed appropriate to introduce them to Paulo Freire's words and his work with Brazilian marginalized population. Soon the students discovered that very close to the Colegio Alexander von Humboldt, although hidden from view by a tall brick wall, there was a small *barriada* and they proposed we could use Freire's ideas to bring literacy to those living there.

The first rude awakening for the students was that the people living in the *barriada* did not speak Spanish so they were not going to be able to become literate in Spanish. Two students who spoke Quichua, proposed to offer literacy in Quichua, but learning to read was not what the people wanted.

And thus, we learned the first lesson, if we indeed wanted to be useful to this population, we first needed to listen to them, to discover what really could be meaningful in their present lives.

Two things surfaced immediately: First, the whole group survived from the money the men earned selling produce on the streets. And the men saw not use in reading letters unless they first learned to understand the value of the different coins and bills and learn how to add and subtract. Until that moment they just extended their hand for the buyer to give them the adequate amount for the vegetable or fruits they offered, but they never knew if they had been given the right amount, just as when they let the customers pick the change from the money they showed them in their hands.

Second, since they had no refrigeration or any way to keep fresh the produce they purchased at the market, they lost what they could not sell quickly. So, they wished they could sell something that would not go bad. Several of the women knew how to sew, but they did not owe a sewing machine.

The students were able to secure three used sewing machines, but how would it be determined who could use them?

Following Freire's *praxis* the students engaged the group in dialogue, with the help of our two interpreters, and interesting outcomes developed. The community decided they needed a community space, where the sawing machines would be kept. Parents of the students provided some building materials and a simple, but perfectly useful community building was created. Then, more dialogue was needed to decide how the sawing machines would be used, until the women came up with the idea of a schedule, that not only would allow everyone to have their turn with the machines, but included time for those who knew how to use the machines to teach the others, and the agreement that they will bring their small children to the community center so that all children would be watched by the mothers who were not sawing, and those working could do it without having to be worried about their children.

One interesting anecdote occurred when the community center was being painted. The people asked the students to paint numbers on their very rustic houses, made mostly of straw mats. But when the students tried to determine in which order the numbers would be painted, the people strongly objected to any order, they each wanted to give their home a number of their choice. Since there was no mail delivery service or any other external reason for the numbers, they simply wanted them because they had seen the houses in the city had numbers.

This simple experience lead us to interesting reflections. Freire explains clearly that the oppressed want to imitate the oppressors, internalizing a desire to be like the oppressors, and eventually becoming oppressors themselves. Having numbers painted on their homes was innocent enough, but the fact that they served no purpose but imitating what was perceived as a form of status was a significant example of how cultures end up assimilated and destroyed.

The most significant thing about this small but meaningful project was that it was all conceived and carried on by the students. Good literature, through strong characters and vivid description of their lives, had moved these young people to see a reality that had been present all along, very close to them, but had for a long time been ignored. Freire's ideas and example had moved them to action.

In critical pedagogy our purpose is to support the growth and liberation of all participants. We understand human liberation as the result of praxis; a process of reflection as a preparation for action, followed by reflecting on the results of our action, which leads us to new insights and therefore to new action, in an ongoing cycle of growth and learning.

An essential part of that learning is a critical analysis of our own culture. In this area, a major influence for me has been the *Unlearning Racism* work of Ricky Sherover-Marcuse. It is good to see that the work of this powerful and inspiring teacher is being carried on by many of her students and colleagues, and that her writings are continuing to be published posthumously, both in print and on Internet (1994, 2000).

In the process of working with and mentoring my own students, the memory of two of my own professors and mentors has been invaluable to me. I maintained a nourishing friendship over the years with Dr. Elena Catena, my professor at the Universidad Complutense in Madrid who first recognized my love for literature, challenged me to greater academic rigor, and from then on, continuously encouraged me to write.

Several years later, I had the opportunity, while a Radcliffe scholar, to attend Dr. Raimundo Lida's courses at Harvard. In the process of transforming my doctoral thesis on the poet Pedro Salinas into a book (1969, 2018), Dr. Lida's comments and suggestions were very helpful. The sincere respect with which he approached my work has remained with me all these years as an inspiring example of how to support another person's research.

Outside of a classroom context, another teacher and mentor has been my late long-time editor and friend Bernice Randall, an outstanding model of clarity, precision, and respect for the written text. From her I learned a great deal about the close relationship that must exist between author and reader if they are to walk, hand in hand, toward a meaningful shared understanding.

Over the years, I have come to realize how much I have been influenced by my own family of educators, especially my grandmother Dolores Salvador de Lafuente. I have written about her in

"Teacher", one of the vignettes in *Where the Flame Trees Bloom* (1994), now included in *Island Treasures* (2016) as an enduring example of how we must not be afraid to acknowledge the central importance of love and care in the learning process.

Recently I have finally been able to publish the book *Dolores Salvador: maestra de maestras* {Dolores Salvador: teachers' teacher] (2018) where I include some of her own writings, unearthed from old publications kept in Cuban libraries, as well as some texts written about her by her own daughters. It has been a great satisfaction to be able to honor her, to whom I owe so much, and also to make her example available to others.

From these various sources, along with my own lifetime of praxis, I have distilled the following principles as central to my own philosophy of education:

- As human beings, we need to love and be loved. Therefore, we learn better in an environment that offers love and respect, and allows us to experience and honor the truth of our thoughts, emotions and feelings.

- As human beings, we are continually learning and creating meaning from our experience. Therefore, we learn better in an environment that allows us to learn at our own pace and in our own way, that honors what we care about, and that builds on what we have already learned from our life experience.

- As human beings, we are vulnerable to, and deeply influenced by, the hurtful aspects of our society. Racism, as well as other forms of prejudice and oppression such as ageism, sexism, ableism, heterosexism, homophobia, anti-Semitism, etc. are pervasive in our world and influence all of us in unconscious ways. Therefore, we need to begin by recognizing prejudice and oppression in order to unlearn them.

- As humans, we are social beings. Therefore, we learn better in an interactive, supportive and non-competitive environment. As we live in a competitive society, it takes intention and effort to establish a co-creative atmosphere.

- All cultures deserve respect, and when understood in their fullness, are usually to be admired. At the same time, all cultures contain some elements that need improvement in order to adequately protect universal human rights. To be most effective, this improvement needs to come from within the culture, or in partnership with it, rather than imposed upon it.

While it is helpful to become clear about the principles that we hold and upon which we base our practice, the point of education is never to "teach" others to parrot our own values. Instead, our work as educators is to help people reflect on their own experiences and those of others, so that they may freely arrive at their own understandings, beliefs, and values.

In the classroom, as in life, praxis begins with reflection upon our past experience, our history, and our present circumstances, as a preparation for action in the present. Our deliberate and considered action is followed in turn by further reflection. *What happened? What was expected, what was predictable, what was new and surprising? What have I learned, and how will that shape and influence the next action that I will take?* And so, reflection is once again followed by action and the cycle continues, with the goal being the full flowering of human freedom, well-being, and creativity.

Our principles therefore need to be embodied in the "learning experiences" —readings, classroom dialogues, action research projects— that we design, assign our students, or invite them to create. In addition, we are also continuously offering students the experience of our example, our own best efforts to live and teach in the light of our principles.

The following guidelines have been helpful reminders for me in this ongoing process of creating helpful learning experiences for my students:

1. Engaging in an on-going exploration

of how I might best live my pedagogical principles, instead of merely talking about them.

2. Fostering a spirit of trust and openness by looking for ways to respond to new and challenging situations as opportunities for learning, instead of responding from fear or a desire for control.

3. Creating opportunities for each student to engage both in individual work and learning as well as in group work and learning.

4. Investing time and effort in the creation of a community of learners by giving people the opportunity to get to know one another and to understand one another's needs and expectations. This allows everyone to feel included, respected, and supported.

5. Ensuring that the teacher is not the only one who gains from students' knowledge, experience and reflections, by developing structures that allow for

the knowledge that is generated or constructed throughout the course to be shared by all.

In exploring these principles and guidelines over the years, I developed a number of classroom practices that served to create an engaged and authentic climate for learning.

Alma Flor Ada

11. Classroom Practices

The following practices are ones that became an established part of my courses. In some cases, the initial suggestions came from students, including the teaching assistants who contributed greatly to the overall strength of the program.

Self-Portraits.

During the first session of a course, I would ask students to briefly introduce themselves to the group, and to afterwards complete written questionnaires about themselves. The purpose of the questionnaires was to gather information to share with the entire class. This was explicitly stated, and students were reminded that any information they wanted to remain confidential needed to be clearly identified as such.

In addition to basic biographical information, I included more personal questions, such as: *Why are you in this course this semester? What would you like to receive from this course (intellectually, academically, socially, personally)? What would you like others in this class to understand and celebrate about you, things that most people would not know unless you told them? What would you like to contribute to others in this class? Is there anything else you would like us to know about you?*

I would then take the questionnaires home and transcribe them. I realize this could now all be done electronically. Yet for me, typing the handwritten questionnaires became an enjoyable way of developing an internal connection with each student.

At the beginning of the next class, each person would receive a complete set of the self-portraits. If many of the students were new and the size of the class permitted it, I would invite students to re-introduce themselves, and to make additional notes about their classmates on the portraits.

An additional activity to facilitate that students develop a deeper understanding of each other was to create **I Am** and **Where I Come From** poems.

These two models of poems do not require much time to be created, and yet can be a most meaningful depiction of a person. The website www.authorsintheclassroom.com describes the process to create them and offers numerous examples. A simple suggestion on how to go about creating them appears in the appendix.

When each student in the class creates one or both of these poems, they can be collected in a book that can become a treasure for the group.

CLASS DIRECTORY. We always found it useful to have a directory with students' names and contact information. Usually one of the students took responsibility for creating it.

WRITTEN REFLECTIONS. Toward the end of each class session, students were asked to complete a page of anonymous feedback and reflections. They were given a few minutes to answer questions such as: *What did I learn today? What was most useful for me? What did other students in the class learn from me today? What questions or concerns do I have now? What would be helpful to me in subsequent classes? What could we do to enrich this class?*

At the top of the page, I included a quote from Maturana and Varela on reflection:

> *"Reflection is a process of knowing how we know. It is an act of turning back upon ourselves. It is the only chance we have to discover our blindness and to recognize that the certainties and knowledge of others are, respectively, as overwhelming and tenuous as our own."* (1987, p. 24).

These pages were then collected and later transcribed, with all of the various responses to each question grouped together. At the beginning of the following class, each student would receive a copy of the compiled set, and we would allocate class time for reading and discussing the feedback.

The value of this process cannot be overemphasized. In addition to helping students reflect upon their own experience of the class and their own learning process, it also helped surface significant differences in background, preferences, and learning styles among the students. In turn, this led to a greater sense of understanding and connection with one another, and a more authentic feeling of community.

It was often quite illuminating for everyone to see how diverse the answers to the first two questions could be. While everyone had attended the same class, seldom did any two individuals report having learned the same thing, nor having found the same experience most useful. This made it clear to everyone that if each person's needs were to be addressed, we would need to learn to understand different perspectives. For example, it often was the case that some students would respond: "keep the small group discussions, we need the opportunity to talk among ourselves" while others would request, "please do not waste class time in student discussions, we want to hear from you."

Initially, when I first began asking students to complete the Class Reflections form, I thought that I was just asking for feedback to allow me to improve the class. Soon, it became apparent that sharing the reflections back with the whole class was a powerful way to generate a greater sense of trust and transparency within the group. It also became a significant learning experience for all of us, as we became more aware of our differences as well as our commonalities.

And it became a clear demonstration of the fallacy of pretending that all students, in any class, be at the same time on the same page with identical results.

CLASS CHRONICLE. Every community process is a historical one, and merits being chronicled. While the written feedback at the end of each session provided a record of student responses to what had occurred in class, the class chronicles offered a summary record of the content of class presentations and discussions.

In addition, the chronicles provided yet another opportunity for reflection on the learning process.

At the beginning of the semester, students were grouped into teams. Part of each team's responsibility included chronicling one or two class sessions. Team members took notes and photos, interviewed other students as needed to report on the highlights of the small-group dialogues, and included in the chronicle any relevant information such as student updates, progress reports on projects, recommended readings, etc.

At the beginning of each session, team members distributed an initial draft of the previous session's chronicle. Students were encouraged to offer comments along with any necessary additions or revisions. As a result, even though the first draft of the chronicle was the product of one team, the final version included the consensus (or if needed the noted dissentions or clarifications) of the entire class.

Initially, the class chronicles began as a way for students to share the burden of note-taking among themselves. Yet as we began to engage in an evolving process of recording our reflections and experiences together, it became clear that what we were doing was not just note-taking, but "making history". This, in turn, strengthened the shared sense of being active agents in our own collective learning experience.

CLASSROOM ENVIRONMENT: OUR GEOGRAPHY. Since history takes place in space as well as in time, it was important for students to take ownership of the space within which their classes took place and to take responsibility for having that space reflect the pedagogy and history of their particular learning community. Frequently tables were moved to form a horse-shoe shape, or chairs were moved to form a circle. Students from each project team would often choose to sit together, so the teams became functional units within the class sessions as well as between sessions.

Students in each course tended to develop their own meaningful décor for making the space "theirs". In some courses, students created collages that incorporated photos of everyone in the class. In others, students created symbolic representations of the principles or social issues under discussion, or created posters with meaningful quotes from the assigned readings. In some classes, students chose to have background music during the class session and selected classical music and folk music from various cultures for that purpose.

While enhancing the classroom environment was not usually part of an assigned project, these initiatives often arose naturally as students took greater ownership of their learning process.

CULTURAL OFFERINGS. Each course included both individual assignments and group assignments. One group assignment was specifically designed to facilitate learning about one another's cultural backgrounds. In addition to the class chronicles, each team was responsible for offering a cultural experience to the rest of their classmates twice during the semester.

This assignment provided an opportunity for a more in-depth exploration of the concept of culture, beyond the more obvious manifestations of food, heroes and holidays to underlying values and worldviews. Of course, food is also important! Since we had long four-hour classes, the team in charge of the cultural sharing was also in charge of bringing edibles to share. This might be dinner for a Friday night class, breakfast for a Saturday morning class, or a snack for Saturday afternoon. While we greatly appreciated the food, and welcomed hearing about what these particular dishes represented within their culture or their family, we also insisted that the cultural sharing go beyond food.

Another helpful learning opportunity took place whenever students, typically from the dominant culture, expressed their concern that they had no culture to share. This provided an opportunity to explore the difficult yet essential concept of ethnocentrism, or how one's own culture can become invisible and unquestioned whenever it is assumed to be the "norm".

JOURNALING. Students were encouraged to keep journals as an individual and private activity. This was the only writing assignment that was designed for the faculty's eyes only. I must confess that having myself been remiss at keeping journals, I initially embraced this activity with some hesitation, and only at the suggestion of an enthusiastic teaching assistant. Yet the positive results that so many students experienced with this process convinced me of its value, and I ended up including it as a regular part of my course assignments.

I found the journals to be as varied as the students. Some were written quickly, with just one thought to synthesize the day, while others were lengthy reflections. Some journals were poetic, others factual.

147

Some students chose to focus on the ups and downs of their daily lives, while others emphasized their intellectual journey. I found them all to be rich and fascinating… and for students who were engaged in participatory research, their journals often became an important research tool and source of information.

INDIVIDUAL CLASS PROJECTS AND GROUP SYNTHESIS. In each class, students were expected to carry out a substantial individual project. These individual projects were also shared with the class, with the help of the various teams. In fact, the task of synthesizing the individual projects and sharing the results with the class was the primary task that students carried out in their teams, and by far the most challenging one.

In each course, the individual project assignment was divided into several sections (usually between four and six) which corresponded roughly to the number of teams in the class. Each class session, a different section of the project was due. Students were asked to bring several copies of their work: one for the professor, one for each teaching assistant, and one for each member of the team whose turn it was to synthesize the individual project section due that week.

Since every student in the class was on a team, this meant that each student, in addition to:

- completing his or her own individual project over the course of the semester;

also:

- read at least one section of each of his or her classmates' projects, as part of a synthesizing team;
- engaged in the challenge of creating, as a team, a written analysis and synthesis of all class members' work on that particular project section;
- developed, as a team, an informative and artistic presentation to share with the class regarding the project section that the team had read, analyzed, and synthesized.

Students generally found this group synthesis to be quite a challenging project. Often, it was the most difficult project they had yet encountered in their academic careers. In some courses, each individual project had a similar theme (for example, "democracy and education", or "first-language maintenance", or "the transmission of cultural heritage") yet each student was working with a unique population that had its own particular characteristics. In other courses, each student project had a different theme, yet the synthesizing team still needed to create a coherent framework and present common threads as well as differences.

While challenging, the process of analyzing the work of their classmates in search of similarities and differences was an extremely valuable opportunity for students to expand their own perspectives. In addition, this kind of reflection and critical thinking helped prepare students to later create a very substantial "review of the literature" section for their own dissertations.

Each team presented, at a later session, the synthesis they had created. This gave the rest of the students the opportunity to learn about the various approaches that others in the class were taking with regard to their individual projects. In turn, this created an opportunity for students to reflect further on their own projects and continue to improve upon them.

12. Reading the World:
A Conference Celebrating Multicultural Literature for Children and Young Adults

Being open to the moment and acknowledging the students' experiences and interests may be the most valuable asset in the teaching/learning process.

While the practices mentioned in the previous chapter proved to be valuable, a moment when I was willing to disregard them created a most significant experience for the students in a given class and for students many years following.

My courses were usually very well attended, yet on a particular semester one of the classes had a very low enrollment. During the process of establishing the course procedures I suggested that since we were not too many, maybe instead of breaking in smaller groups we could consider having the whole class work together in a project, if we could find one that would interest everyone.

Students began brainstorming with those sitting close by, when one of them, Beverly Vaughn Hock, raised her hand to make a proposal. She explained that Dr. Marilyn Nye, a Professor of Children's Literature at the California State University East Bay (Hayward at that time) was retiring. Upon her retirement *The Celebration of Children's Literature Conference*, a significance event for teachers and librarians in the Bay Area, which Dr. Nye organized every year, was to be discontinued. Would we as a class want to take responsibility for keeping this conference going?

The class became very busy discussing this proposal. Initially there did not seem to be much of an echo for this idea. Taking over the organization of this event seemed like a big responsibility and most of the students already had very demanding full-time jobs. Also, while a couple of them shared Bev's interest in children's literature this was not really an interest for most. The course focus was Linguistics in Education and most of the students were focused on developing or improving bilingual education and second language acquisition. Then, someone commented: "We are an International Multicultural Program, so if we were to consider organizing this conference it should have a multicultural focus." And she went on to elaborate how multicultural books that would give an authentic representation of diversity were absent from most classroom experiences.

This shift in the conversation, from taking over an event most of them had never known about, and turn it into an opportunity to discover, study, and disseminate information about quality books of particular significance to the populations they served led to a decision that enriched substantially the International Multicultural Program, IME as we refer to it.

The students named the conference appropriately *Reading the World*, referring both to the fact that it would focus on books reflecting the World's diversity and also acknowledge Paulo Freire's philosophy that besides reading words it is necessary to learn to read the World, that is, the reality we live in and its social conditions in order to transform them.

During its ten years of existence *Reading the World* became the most significant conference on children's and young adult literature West of the Mississippi and one of the most significant in the nation. Dr. Jack Zipes, a World-wide highly respected scholar in the study of fairy tales claimed "it was the best conference he had ever attended."

Organized by students with the collaboration of local librarians and children's literature enthusiastic, *Reading the World* programs were always surprisingly rich. Each conference offered, besides a diversity of workshops and small session, seven remarkable key note speakers. These speakers represent a rich variety of authors and illustrators from different backgrounds and ethnicity, providing vast opportunities for students and attendees to learn from and interact with many points of view.

Not only was the quality and number of speakers remarkable for a weekend conference, but the fact that the speakers committed to be present during the full length of the conference was unique. The usual practice of most conference is that the key-note speakers have minimal participation after their speech.

At *Reading the World* is was common that after their own presentation, the speakers would join the audience and participate alongside the students and general public. This created real opportunities for dialogue that contributed to the building of a true sense of community, so much so that many of the authors and scholars who gave key note presentations returned on various other occasions, as did workshop leaders and presenters.

Held at the School of Education building in the University of San Francisco campus, *Reading the World* always had a friendly nature. While the presenters were offered lunch at a private location many chose to have their lunch in open spaces alongside the students and general public sharing on the festive atmosphere.

Dr. Beverly Vaughn Hock, which remained the conference's key driving force, became an Adjunct Professor and every year taught a Fall semester course devoted to studying the work of the main presenters of the conference to be held that Spring. Students were assigned a speaker of a workshop presenter to host throughout the three days as guides and assistants.

The students were given the opportunity to become intimately acquainted with the body of work of each speaker All keynote speakers and presenters were introduced by students who had studied their work in depth and were always pleasantly surprised by the meaningful introductions and grateful to have such well-informed audience.

Often the break out sessions were headed by figures who normally were keynote speakers in their own right such as **Francisco Jiménez, Margaret McElderry, Effie Lee Morris, Suni Paz, Aaron Shepherd, Robert San Souci, Ashley Wolff**, and **Diane Wolkstein.**

Looking at the presenters in retrospect it is of particular significance to me that *Reading the World* offered a platform and recognition to many of today's well-known Latino authors at a time when they were beginning their careers. Alongside with the already consecrated Latino authors who offered keynote speeches:

> **Francisco Alarcón,**
> **George Ancona,**
> **Isabel Campoy,**
> **Pat Mora,**
> **Yuyi Morales,** and
> **Gary Soto**

the students at the University of San Francisco and the *Reading the World* attendees were enriched by the opportunity to listen to the emergent voices of:

> **Jorge Argueta,**
> **Mónica Brown,**
> **Rene Colato Laínez,**
> **Margarita Engle,**

**Maya Christina González,
Reyna Grande,** and
Juan Herrera.

One year we worked with the International Board on Books for Young People [IBBY} and put on a joint conference. Another year, representatives of the International Children's Digital Library presented a panel on outstanding books in original and translated editions.

A very significant event, complementing the 1999 conference was the exhibit *From the Wonderful Wizard of Oz to Grandfather's Journey 20th Century Illustrations for Children's Literature* curated by F. Isabel Campoy at the Thacher Gallery in the USF Gleeson Library.

The exhibit presented both remarkable books and originals illustrations of children's books.

The books include first and exceptional editions of the Oz books, from the Rare Book Collection of the USF Library, as well as early 20th century special editions of children's literature books from the personal collection of Dr. Julia Marshall, professor of Art at San Francisco State University, at the time an IME doctoral student.

The original illustrations included works from national and international award winning illustrators: **George Ancona, Willi Baum, Armando Cepeda, Remy Chaplin, Hilario Cruz, Felipe Dávalos, Julie Downing, Jason Dryg, Viví Escrivá, Maya Cristina González, Susan Guevara, Thacher Hurd, Elisa Kleven, Michael Lacapa, Héctor Viveros Lee, Ileana Lee, Antonio Martorell, Gerald McDermott, Emanuel Paniagua, Joe Sam, Daniel Sans Souci, Allen Say, Simón Silva, Leslie Tryon, Ashley Wolff, Yolanda Garfias Woo.**

At every conference we offered a platform for storytellers from a variety of cultures to engage with the audience.

The *Reading the World Award,* was conferred in recognition of the support of outstanding contributions of making quality literature accessible to children and young adults.

The *Reading the World Award* recipients were:

Ashley Bryan, F. Isabel Campoy, Anita De Frantz, Francisco Jiménez, Milly Lee, Effie Lee Morris, Marilyn E. Nye, Ruth Stotter, and **Jack Zipes.**

Some of the authors became enthusiastic supporters of the conference and would return to present, over and again. Knowing that while held at the University, the Conference needed to be self-supportive, some authors generously offered to have their publishers cover their expenses and honorarium. Among these supporters who I will always remember with immense gratitude were **Arnold Adoff, Ashley Bryan, Gerald McDonald** and **Jack Zipes**.

My gratitude goes also to the exceptional authors, illustrators and scholars who, as keynote speakers, offered inspiration and insights to the students and all the *Reading the World* attendees, among them:

**Arnold Adoff,
Francisco Alarcón,
George Ancona,**

Joseph Bruchac,
Isabel Campoy,
Leo & Diane Dillon,
Nancy Farmer,
Debra Frazier,
Nancy Garden,
Nikki Giovanni,
Virginia Hamilton,
Herbert Kohl,
Michael Lacapa,
Ana María Machado,
Ken Mochizuki,
Pat Mora,
Yuyi Morales,
Marilyn Nelson,
Naomi Shihab Nye,
Linda Sue Park,
 Pat McKissack,
Katherine Paterson,
Ann Pellowski,
Gay Ross,
Allen Say,
Peter Sis,
Gary Soto,
Leslie Tryon,
Rosemary Wells,
Virginia Euwer Wolff,
Laurence Yep,
Junko Yokota,

**Jane Yolen,
Ed Young.**

The following words from Beverly Vaughn Hock offer a brief summary from the person who was the soul of the conference from beginning to end:

Amazing connections, lasting friendships, and unexpected new projects grew out of *Reading the World, a Conference Celebrating Multicultural Literature for Children and Young Adults*.

The conference became both a wonderful explosion of full- blown academic insights and adventures and a warm, lively party celebration of creativity.

To read more about the conference and see description of the programs, including both keynotes and workshops, information on presenters, the Reading the World award recipients, etc. visit:
www.almaflorada.com/reading-the-world-conference/

13. Sharing vs Appropriating Knowledge
Teotitlán del Valle, Oaxaca

A constant concern for me has been always that my actions would not perpetuate the structures of power. In teaching this meant to be sure that I would not be the sole beneficiary of the students' work and learning.

At the High School level in Lima, I made sure students shared with the class the books they read commenting what the reading has meant personally for them and highlighting how it could be of interest to other students. I could see the impact this had on widening the students' interest to books they otherwise may not have chosen to read.

It was also important for me to validate their voices, publishing their writings and to analyze their creations with the same detail and respect used to analyze the writings of notable authors. My goal was to contribute to develop students respect for each other and also emphasize the equal respect deserved by all human beings.

The original publications were humble mimeographed copies, eventually their writings would be included in the books on writing I was publishing, *Ver y describir y Oír y narrar*. Some students were interested in photography and contributed photos taken by them to the books.

The issue of being the sole beneficiary of the students learning became highly significant while teaching at the graduate and doctoral level. The evolution of technology facilitates sharing information and I am pleased to see that students in some graduate programs, are encouraged to share digitally their papers with each other. This certainly was not available at the time I was teaching, but for me it was imperative that I would not be the only one benefiting from the research and thoughts of the students in my classes.

Encouraging self-publication, shared in the classroom was the beginning to creating pathways that would lead to becoming formally published authors.

When empowered to speak their minds and hearts, students were not only willing but excited to accept my suggestion that presentations needed to go beyond reading aloud their papers, and instead would make the information come alive by resourcing to art and creativity so that the audience would not only receive rich and diverse information, but would do so in most enjoyable, dynamic and participatory ways.

There would be many rich examples that could be shared to this respect: I can think of Annie Rodríguez Torres dissertation defense. She brought a series of different flowering plants to beautifully represent each of the women who had been her participants. In this way she protected the identity of her participants, Latina mothers who had spent time in prison, while giving us a living image of each of their personalities.

And I will never forget the excitement we experienced when, on a teaching Saturday, students found signs on the walls of the School of Education announcing the presence of Paulo Freire, which in reality turned out to be a puppet show, using archived voice recordings of Paulo. This experience is described in full in the chapter 15, Paulo Freire Scholarship.

The precious puppet now greets visitors at the Paulo Freire Archive at Chapman University. And the memory of Guadalupe Solis' clever idea to use puppetry to present and comment on some of Freire's ideas continues to make me smile.

Giving students the opportunity to hear and dialogue with some of the scholars they were reading seemed of paramount importance to me.   Since there was no university budget for this, I had to resource to creative ways to invite some of them to our classes.

Having extremely generous friends who had their own means to come to San Francisco and volunteered to speak in my classes allowed my students, through the years, to listen to María Torres Guzmán, Mary Popplin, Stephen Krashen and Cathy Walsh. A long negotiation with the Fulbright Scholar Exchange program led to an invitation to Dr. Valeria Kukharenko, from the University of Odessa, to spend an academic year at USF.

Later I discovered that I could teach a course beyond my own teaching load and request that the money owned me for the extra work would be used to pay visiting scholars. This allowed my students to interact in the classroom with notable scholars like, among others, Robert Phillipson and Tove Skutnabb-Kangas.

Dialogue and interactions with these scholars provided student's with opportunities to enrich their research through new ideas for projects. One moment which ignited interest, and began a long string of profound research projects, publications and dissertations, happened during one of Tove Skuttnab-Kangas' visits.

Tove challenged the class with the question: *What are the worst things that can happen if children lose their mother tongue?* This question lead to powerful dialogue, and collectively the class decided to produce, individually or in small groups, praxis-based pamphlets designed to describe to various populations, parents, teachers, educational administrators and leader, the consequences of Language Loss.

One particularly long lasting and poignant example from that work was the dissertation and extended Linguistic Genocide research and projects of Nancy Jean Smith. Rather than describe this experience solely in my words I have asked Dr. Nancy Jean to contribute her memories to this chapter, and with her usual generosity she agreed. This is how she describes the beginning of the process:

While working as a Title VII Bilingual Specialist I would visit bilingual classes throughout the California Central Valley to work with small groups of children.

*I chose to start a project with a small group of 3rd grade girls, asking them, "**What did it feel like when you did not speak English?**" The girls illustrated their feelings using art materials, and I encouraged them to put the many feelings showed by their pictures into words, in order to talk about them.*

*At some point, one of the girls said very quietly: "**Maestra, no solo tuvimos que aprender inglés, también tuvimos que aprender español**".* [Teacher, not only did we have to learn English, we also had to learn Spanish.]

Nancy Jean continues:

"What happened next was to have a lifelong and lasting impact, not only for me and my family, but also for thousands of immigrant families, educators and their families, on both sides of the border and beyond.

*This moment began a series of wonderful events when the student slowly whispered, "**Hablamos Zapoteco.**"* [Our language is Zapotec.]

171

Having lived in indigenous communities in Southern Mexico, Nancy Jean quickly realized the students were part of an extended Zapotec community throughout the Central Valley of California. Using the Creative Dialogue Methodology described in Chapter 2 and the Participatory Research process, a pamphlet was produced with Spanish and English versions: *¿Cómo se siente uno cuando no habla inglés?* and **How does it feel when you don't speak English?** Initially they were distributed by the girls throughout the school and the community. Later they were shared by Nancy Jean in conferences and publications.

"Through this project" Nancy Jean says *"it became apparent how little teachers knew or understood of these children's lives. "*

During this time Nancy Jean was invited by another doctoral student, Kristin Brown, who was studying the binary reality of Puerto Rican students who spend part of their lives in the United States and part in Puerto Rico.

"*There, at the University of Puerto Rico,* "Nancy Jean says, *"I was able to observe the development of Kristin's doctoral research in a bilingual, binational setting around many of the same immigrant issues that I was uncovering."*

Nancy Jean returned from Puerto Rico to her school community and shared the work that the New York and Puerto Rican teachers were collaboratively undertaking. She writes: *"I explained how the teachers came together to better understand their binational students' needs. Some Zapotec parents immediately saw the power of that project and how a similar project could benefit their community. They asked me if a Binational Project could be set up in their village of Teotitlán del Valle.*

So, Nancy Jean made a visit to Teotitlán del Valle in Oaxaca. That visit convinced her how helpful it would be for teachers to have a first-hand experience of the richness of the students' culture and its substantive differences from what they encounter in a Californian classroom. This culminated in the conception of *The Seminar on*

Transformative Literacy, an educational and cultural summer immersion experience for teachers and their families and friends, that ran for 12 years, and became the month-long, **SEP Binational Teacher Exchange Project.** Sponsored by the Secretaría de Educación Pública de Mexico [SEP], the equivalent to the Mexican National Office of Education, the program was recognized on both sides of the border.

Isabel and I accompanied Nancy Jean and a group of 38 educators during the first summer. Immediately upon our arrival to the village, we were received by a marching band and an ensemble of *Danzantes*, village dancers along with dancing children. The dancers were all impressively dressed in colorful authentic indigenous garb. We were marched in a procession of pomp and color, and with great respect to the village municipal plaza.

There the whole community awaited, presided over by the council of elders, the village president and his cabinet. Then, using a loud microphone A young man,

Andrés Bautista, who held the position of "The Village Voice", translated the elders' greetings.

"Welcome... So, here again, foreigners. What do they want to take from us this time?" After the lively music and the smiles on the dancing children's faces, these booming, resounding words filled the plaza as a shocking reminder of the inequity between our two worlds, of the many hundreds of years of humiliation, oppression, trickery and bigotry.

Mindful of this vast difference in economics and culture, Nancy Jean had been very explicit that this experience should be beneficial to the village. None of the workshop leaders would be receiving any payment and all the fees for the course would be gifted to the village in one way or another. We were asked to donate school supplies and books, had procured musical instruments for the children's band, and donated the village's first computer. A schedule was created that provided private tutoring on the computer every day we were there. Besides, we would all be staying in private homes and paying for our lodging and food.

Nevertheless, the words we heard clearly put us on notice, reminded us of what not only Zapotec, but all Mesoamerican Indians have experienced historically and unfortunately continue to experience in a myriad of ways to this day. We felt awe and respect for the long history, culture, and language of the people of Teotitlán, and for the fact that they were so proudly standing up to us and all that had been taken from them by those that came before us.

Most archeologists date the founding of Teotitlán del Valle back to the time of the first settlers in the Central Valley of Oaxaca, some 14,000 years ago. That fact alone is pause for respect and humbleness, and everyone there would grow to understand the deep and historical meaning of what was being put before us.

The major source of income in Teotitlán comes from producing and selling their hand-woven rugs from the wool of the sheep they raise. The village awakens daily to the rhythmic sound of the looms from almost every home.

The beautifully intricate designs they created are inspired from the age-old artwork of their ancestors, pulled from deep in their hearts, as they explained to us. Yet, they suffer the exploitation of the sellers who buy their product paying very low prices.

Navajo blankets are highly priced in the States, so the sellers had conceived a scheme that robs both communities. Weavers from Teotitlán are asked to leave aside their traditional designs and colors and substitute them with Navajo colors and designs. The products can still be labeled as hand-crafted by indigenous hands. By omitting that those hands do not belong to the Navajo, the products are sold at the high prices the Navajo have been able to achieve for their work, while the weavers from Teotitlán are paid substantially less.

Another form of exploitation takes place when the buyers refuse to honor the price they had originally agreed to pay on large orders. The weavers, who have already invested time and wool, do not have the economic capacity to refuse the lower price and have to sell for whatever the buyers are willing to pay.

Unquestionably the elders had reasons for mistrusting us.

This has been one of the most difficult moments in my career. I could see the confusion in the faces of the committed teachers from the United States that had embarked on this experience with all best of intentions. Foremost in their minds was to learn from the villagers how to best serve their students and communities... And now, a mirror was put up to all our faces, exposing our individual and collective ignorance of what this village has actually endured. It was clear that our journey was pending on our response, and on my very words.

All I could say was the truth, so I affirmed to the elders that they were right, that they had every reason to be suspicious of foreigners. We had indeed come to take something away, we only needed them to know that what we had come for was knowledge. What they had, and we wanted to take, would be a treasure to us, but we could assure them that the treasure of knowledge would be used to benefit the children of their community, and similar communities, that had been entrusted to these educators. I told them that our most passionate commitment was to contribute to create a better, just, and inclusive world. Most importantly, I acknowledged that we knew we were not fit to educate their children unless we learned from them.

Their answer was as skeptical as their greeting: "We shall see when we say good-bye to you what we think of what you have come to do."

That month in Teotitlán allowed for profound experiences and beautiful memories. One of the participants, Ryan James, made a self-published picture book for his students in the United States and he called it *El maestro tonto* (The Foolish Teacher). He used this expression at the beginning of each page to explain he was the foolish teacher, since he had not known basic things about the culture of his students, and he named and illustrated the things he had learned, one per page.

Recognizing to our students what we don't know is a liberating way of letting them know that everyone of us —no matter our age, or previous schooling— knows very little when we sum up all that can be known in the World. If we consider the sum of human knowledge in all fields, science and art, of all languages and their literature, the knowledge is so vast not even one of the Nobel Prize Winners would have reached kindergarten. And yet, so often with a narrow view point we establish prestige and vast differences between those who know a little bit more than others, forgetting we are all learners.

Nancy Jean states: *We often forget to include the idea that "we are all learners", the fact that we all have something new to learn, in our learning processes and daily interactions. We never know when new knowledge will be presented to us, nor in what packet it will come. We learned and were reminded daily from the families and the community of Teotitlán del Valle that knowledge comes in many different packages, and many different forms, and the best way to be in the world is as a learner.*

What Nancy Jean expresses is what I have always tried to demonstrate through my teaching to find every new way to "Listen Loudly", as mentioned in Chapter 5.

Another of the participating teachers, Richard Keis joined the doctoral program after that summer. He went on to develop in Oregon an outstanding program for migrant farm working parents. *Libros y familias*, developed critical awareness through discussing children's books and in turn having the parents writing their own books to share their ideas.

Talented Sylvia Dorta Duque de Reyes, who has been a loving collaborator throughout my life in California, organized a representation by the village children of my book *The Gold Coin* in the village municipal plaza during the *Despedida*, the Farewell Program that concluded the seminar.

The children, directed by Silvia, created a circular staging around the plaza, to represented the circular character of the narrative. They built doña Josefa's hut and re-created with live plants and natural materials the various sceneries. The whole village attended their amazing performance.

Nancy Jean continued to organize summer courses in Teotitlán. And eventually was able to join the Mexican national "Binational Teacher Exchange Project." Each summer a small group of Oaxacan teachers from the primary and secondary school in Teotitlán, received Oaxacan state support to visit schools in California.

She explains: "*As the Oaxacan and California teachers planned together on how to best serve their students, greater understanding developed on both sides of the border. The collaboration between teachers from both countries grew stronger and lasting relationships developed especially as many of the teachers repeated their experience of visiting the other country. Many of the participating Oaxacan teachers moved into leadership positions at all levels throughout the Oaxacan region, as have many of the United States educators, ensuring the continuation of the work of generating inclusion collaboratively."*

The farewell, again, in the village plaza, was very moving. By then, we had developed friendships with the families that had hosted us in their homes. We had created strong ties, with the parents of the children with whom we worked, with the multiple individuals who had been trained in the use of the computer, with the committee that worked in the library where we left not only the books we brought to donate but also the books we wrote, with the village president and his municipal committee, and with the teachers and principals at the primary and secondary schools.

And again, the elders spoke through "the Village Voice". They acknowledged that we had been different from other people who had come before us, and we would always be welcome back.

Yes, we took many treasures from Teotitlán. I am pleased to know they have been put to good use.

14. Anti-bias education on behalf of the Roma in Eastern Europe

The conference room was lighted by the summer sun in the Bulgarian resort of Albena. The audience eyes were firmly focused on us, as the participants listened attentively to the words of our translators, but the attitude and body work responses were totally contrary to what we could have expected. Where we waited for acceptance, we saw frowns, when we expected empathy or compassion, the expressions were sarcastic, and when we asked a question the answers made no sense.

Many nights, during my long life as a public speaker, I have had nightmares with being in a situation where the audience is blocked by columns, or I have to speak in an L shaped room where I can't look at both sides of the audience, and, long time ago, before I became comfortable with nudity by living in a clothes optional community, I would even had nightmares of having to speak without clothes.

But none of my nightmares could equal the sense of impotence I felt at the beginning of that course in Bulgaria.

Some of the many significant projects I found myself sharing with students were initiated in the classroom, like *Reading the World*, or were born of a student's research interest like the one conducted at Teotitlán del Valle, in other instances, a project initiated outside the university became a topic of students' interest, and even dissertation topics, like the Pájaro Valley project or the Authors in the Classroom process.

One significant case in which students took over and continued a work which Isabel Campoy and I had initiated in the field was the work on behalf of Roma populations, in Eastern Europe and the Baltic countries supported by George Soros' Open Society Foundation.

George Soro's interest in supporting the education and development of the Roma people, as well as other marginalized populations in Eastern Europe, lead to a conference held in Budapest organized by Elizabeth Lorant and Susan Rona on behalf of the Soros Open Society Foundation. Isabel Campoy and I were invited to participate along with other Anti-Bias educators from Europe and the United States to consider viable possibilities of working on behalf of the Roma to ameliorate an extremely untenable situation of oppression.

As a result of that first encounter, Isabel and I were asked to develop a series of trainings in Hungary, the Czech Republic and Bulgaria in support of the Roma Project, a project meant to improve the education received by Roma children through anti-bias practices and transformative pedagogy. Our goal was to motivate educators to develop a just approach in the education of Roma children and demonstrate via research, that Roma children can learn as well as mainstream children when the educational conditions are right.

Part of the process would include creating a curriculum that would empower the Roma children, their teachers and aides, and the Roma community at large, in order that the students would be able to join mainstream educational institutions and have an opportunity to join successfully the mainstream workforce and society.

As part of a group of educators tasked with putting their heads together to find solutions for the Roma, we visited Roma settlements, schools and informative institutions.

In the Museum dedicated to the Roma created by George Soros in Budapest we visually saw how industrialization and technological advanced had hurt the Roma depriving them of the trades that had previously been their means of support giving them means of contributing to society.

When the three Roma ancestral trades: the raising and domestication of horses, the production and repair of copper pots and other copper objects, and their role as required and celebrated musicians in weddings and celebrations, were made obsolete by technology, the Roma faced the disappearance of opportunities to work on their traditional skills. Racism had kept them marginalized for centuries, and only those traditional skills made them tolerable to a bigoted mainstream population.

Under the Soviet Union regime all children were expected to attend school, but once these rules were not in order, Roma children were no longer welcomed in most schools, where they were forced to sit at the back of the room, separated from the rest of the children at the request of mainstream parents.

The situation became complicated by the fact that in some Eastern European countries to enroll in high school students need to also be apprenticed in a trade. Unfortunately, even the few Roma children able to finished elementary school were faced with the long held racist prejudice against them, making it almost impossible for them to be accepted for apprenticeships and therefore unable to enroll in High School.

On our second trip, we were asked to work in the Czech Republic, Hungary and Bulgaria.

We visited a school in Prague with a great reputation of working well with Roma students. At the end of the visit we had a meeting with the Principal and Vice-Principal and there the sadness of the full truth was revealed. Yes, their elementary students did well and many students completed their elementary schooling, but, alas, when it came to finding placements for them to continue studying all doors were closed. After having visited many places of work, reasoned and begged, they had indeed only been able to find apprenticeship for two students of the elementary graduating class... both in the kitchen of their own school!

In Bulgaria we were to address a particular situation with the only schools that were actively seeking Roma students: these were schools designed for students with serious learning impairments.

During the Soviet period, children with learning challenges of any sort were placed in specialized institutions as boarding students. After the regime change, parents began looking at education models in the United States and requested that children with special needs be integrated into regular classrooms.

The specialized boarding schools lost a great many of their students, except for very severe cases. The personnel of those schools realizing that, without students, they were destined to extinction, decided to recruit the only children available: Roma children.

They lured the parents, striving with poverty, with the promise that in the boarding schools the children would be welcomed, they would be fed and given uniforms, and would receive a special education.

What they did not explained to the parents was that the specialization of their staff was not for working with children of diverse culture and language. That while their speech therapists knew how to treat students with hearing and/or speech impairment they had no clue about how to teach a second language to a child fluent in their native language, as was the case of the Roma children.

The dismaying result was that the Roma children were pretty much ignored in the classrooms and teachers concentrated in the few children they were well equipped to treat. And most Roma children would still remain illiterate and with very limited language skills in the national languages. When these schools appealed to the Soros Foundation for funds, it was explained to them that funds would be available, but only if the Roma children in their care made academic progress.

In order to assist the schools, the Foundation organized various types of training in Second Language Acquisition and Education, but it had become apparent that, without addressing the deeply negative attitudes of the schools' personnel towards the Roma, there would be little perspectives of success.

Working with teams of selected personnel, which usually included the Principal, Assistant Principal, Psychologist and Speech Therapist of special schools from several countries, was our task.

Reflecting about a difficult topic as racism through translators was not easy, particularly when we were able to ascertain the translators' rejection of the Roma was making them distort what we were saying.

In Hungary we had the opportunity of developing a good relationship with the young teacher acting as translator. He had never interacted personally with a member of the Roma community, and yet held all the stereotypes and mistrusts that had been fed to him by his parents and society. The fact that in a few days we had interacted with more Romas in his country than he had in his whole life was an eye-opener to him and he was willing to listen and represent us truthfully.

In Bulgaria we needed to fire the two translators. After the first couple of hours we took a break and checked with the members of the Soros Foundation that were accompanying us, because we were concerned that the audience was reacting in complete dissonance to what we were saying. In the group there were two Bulgarians, both Roma, one of them the first Roma to have obtained a doctorate in education, the other a young teacher. They corroborated our suspicions, the translators were not translating what we were saying, but rather expressing their own disregard for Romas.

We were able to convince them to become our translators, but asked them to begin by telling their own personal stories. This, indeed, changed the audience attitude who listened respectfully to their life stories, sometimes showing real interest and surprise at what they were hearing.

Nevertheless, although we had been able to elicit some interaction with the group, we remained concerned. The course was taking place on a resort by the Baltic, but while we were all staying at the same hotel, the language barrier, since none of the participants spoke English and we did not speak Bulgarian, made it difficult to have meaningful interactions outside of the class. We exchanged smiles but that was pretty much the extent of it. We were mortified that even during meals we had been placed at different ends of the dining room.

The participants had engaged, although somewhat timidly, in the anti-biased education activities and authoring exercises we had proposed. Yet, we still felt very concerned: the back and forth translation took much time, and limited the quality of the responses since we were afraid many nuances were being lost.

So, on Wednesday evening we had a
meeting with the organizers to share our
worries and dismay. Were we truly
reaching the group? Was there anything
different we could be doing? The long
conversation did not result in   many
suggestions and we decided that the only
thing to do was to begin Thursday's class
by directly asking the participants if we
should we be doing things differently.

But when we entered the classroom on the
next morning, we had no need to ask
questions, the students were all ready with
their answers.

One of the long walls of the meeting room
had been covered with the brown paper
silhouette of a tree whose branches
extended along the wall. On the many
branches there were flowers, fruits, and
even some bird nests. On each of them, a
letter.

We stood astonished and moved. The
construction of that mural must had taken
many hours of planning and work.

With moist eyes we asked the translators to tell the participants we would like to know what the letters said.

One by one the participants stood up to read their letters. Some were brief statements of gratitude for having been given the opportunity to see their reality in a new light. Some detailed expressions of their own personal experiences with biases, both the ones they had suffered and the ones they know recognized having held. Some included reflections on the social conditions they saw around them that perpetuated prejudice. Many stated firmly the future actions they had decided to take.

While we agonized about finding ways to reach them, the participants had created the bridge both through art and by accepting our encouragement to use their voices.

Those two summers spent in Eastern Europe were extraordinary experiences for us.

When the Soros Foundation decided to continue offering the trainings, this time in several sites, we were pleased to recommend some of my former students, who were especially well qualified to continue the work. Dr. Jacqueline Reza, who had been my advisee and teacher assistant was asked to chair the group. She was joined by Nancy Jean Smith, whose work in Oaxaca is described in the previous chapter and by Edgar Lampkin, another of the IME graduates.

One of my advisees, Dawn Tankersley had been working for the Soros Foundation in Macedonia, a work which allowed her to write her dissertation, defended in 1999: *Language as Resource for Peace: Critical Reflections on Bridging Two Cultures in a Dual Language Immersion Program in Macedonia.*

Nancy Jean says of the work in which she participated:

Together we had written a Primary Curriculum, but decided that an Adult Curriculum was needed to flush out the biases, as the adults' biases were appearing in the teaching of the Primary Curriculum. The Adult Curriculum workshops were successfully implemented in every country in Eastern Europe except Ukraine, Poland and Belarus. After years of implementation, the trainings that had been initially exclusively under the auspices of the Soros Step by Step offices, to be also implemented by Serbian trainers and combined with their own materials and training.

In each of the countries, local trainers were trained through Trainer of Trainer Trainings and eventually each country took over their own trainings. That was the goal, and we reached that goal.

These trainings took, and still take, great courage to implement, and the work still remains to be done in many countries. Roma assistants have now become Roma teachers in Bulgaria, and other countries, although still in very few.

We just never know when we set out where our work will take us, or what it will look like over time. There are still many educators working diligently to create spaces for Roma and other

minorities to learn mainstream curriculum.
The work that we did gives them hope, courage
and faith to this day.

The issues of oppression faced by people in
Eastern Europe are multiple. Jackie Reza
summarizes them in one of her reports
saying:

Points of oppression center on racism, sexism
and nationalism. Where the Roma are
concerned, oppression is often manifested via
religion and nationality. There is strong Anti-
Semitism but it does not affect jobs or education
at all. It is more of a skinhead type problem. In
other countries oppression manifests itself as
nationalism and culture. For example, you can
have lived in Serbia for 4 or 5 generations but,
if your family was originally from Albania,
then your considered Albanian. And we all
know what that attitude led to — ethnic
cleansing.

Indeed, the issues are of life and death. In
another report, Jackie describes visually a
situation that exemplify how prejudice can
lead to life-destroying situations:

During this last International OSI Institute the Slovak teams had put together a video of a little girl going to school. She lives in a community called Jarovnice. It is on the banks of a small river that flooded two years ago where 80 Roma, most of them old people and children, died in the flood as their "houses" i.e., hovels, went down the river. They live totally segregated on the banks of the river without electricity nor sewage... The major, representing the racist attitudes of the town, will not offer any solutions to their living conditions.

All the Roma children in the town go to the special school. The principal of the school is a professor of special education who chooses to work in this slum and fight for these people. She is a real ally or advocate for the people and they love her and trust her because she delivers.

The 7 minutes movie is not voiced, but does have music and is visually strong. At the beginning one see the little girl talking with a woman. That woman is one of the Roma family coordinators and was encouraging the girl and her family to let her go to the school. When you view the video, you will see what compels me to continue with the project.

The composite evaluation of the *Institute Education for Social Justice. Training the Trainer* conducted in Albena, Bulgaria on July 2003, contains some interesting observations of what participants had gained, beyond the theories, principles and techniques, and experiential practice for conducting trainings that were the stated goals.

They write about the importance of having received *love and support in many ways, that promote holding on, staying committed and not trying to escape.*

Many appreciated the combination of theory and practice and one point highlighted by many was summarized as *having developed awareness of the interconnection of heart and brain — emotions and cognition, knowledge about oppression background— hurts and behavior of individuals connected with these hurts.*

Many participants related that a most significant contribution of the training was being able to observe Jackie, Nancy Jean, and Edgar. Their work as a team surprised and caused admiration and became inspirational for those not used to work in team. They also commented with appreciation on how the facilitators dealt with the patterns of oppression (anger, hate, sadness) and were able to separate the behavior and the person.

Also acknowledged and valued was how the facilitators studied in advance with respect the participants' opinions and were prepared to expect the psychological impact the work would have on the participants.

All of us that would like to contribute to make the world a more inclusive, equitable, and just place for all, have many demands on our efforts. Eventually Jackie, Nancy Jean, Dawn and Edgar found other focus for their work, but I am convinced that the effective work they did on training many Eastern Europeans to work towards social justice in their own communities must have bloomed and bear many fruits.

And, since the work for achieving just and inclusive societies continues to require much effort, in 2019, after an 8-year hiatus, Dr. Nancy Jean Smith has re-initiated work in Budapest in collaboration with a Hungarian educator initially trained as one of the original Adult Curriculum trainers. But this is a new story that Nancy Jean will have to tell.

15. Paulo Freire Scholarship at the IME Program at the University of San Francisco

At the time of my retirement a group of my kind and generous former students planned to organized a scholarship on my name. I suggested that the scholarship be, instead, named after Paulo Freire whose thinking and work has meant so much to all of us. And, thus, the plans to endow a scholarship at USF began.

It took effort and the generosity of many, for this permanent scholarship to become a reality. Special acknowledgement is owed to Dr. Susan Katz, Chair of the IME Program and Dr. Peter Baird, a graduate from IME.

Below is the text of the interview where I was asked to speak about the scholarship. It is accompanied by the lyrics of a song, composed by Peter, recognizing Paulo's significance in the struggle for a better world This song has enlivened many of our gatherings at USF.

Interview from USF on April 5, 2018.

1. Can you share about your history of working with Paulo Freire, what you worked on together, how he became such an influencing force for you in the way you established/structured the IME department?

I began reading the work of Paulo Freire when I was a teacher, working on my PhD in Lima Perú, in the 60s. Students who attended Freire's classes and lectures in Chile transcribed and mimeographed them and some would reach us in Lima. Freire was in exile in Chile, expelled from Brazil by a repressive dictatorship. Later, while still in Lima I was able to find a very rustic paperback edition of *The Pedagogy of the Oppressed*.

I shared Paulo's ideas with my high school students at the Alexander von Humboldt school in Lima, and we began a small project to implement some of Freire's experiences in a small *barriada*, a shanty town in the outskirts of Lima.

After moving to San Francisco in 1976, to teach at USF, I had the opportunity to meet Freire for the first time in a private gathering in Sacramento. He was very warm and welcoming to me, because a common friend: the Peruvian philosopher Augusto Salazar Bondy, had spoken to Freire about me. We were both very sad at that moment by Augusto's untimely death and I believe those feelings contributed to create an immediate bond.

Not long afterwards, Dr. Martin Carnoy, organized a seminar in Stanford for professors and scholars interested in Paulo Freire's work, and invited me to participate.

It was a major experience with about twelve extraordinary people with a great deal of commonality in our thinking.

Freire's first wife, Elsa, accompanied him and sat quietly knitting at one end of the room. Since she did not speak English, the language of the room, I tried to keep her company whenever I could, and, with my limited knowledge of Portuguese and her understanding of Spanish, after having lived in Chile, we managed to create a bond between two Latin American women, with children of similar ages, who had known the difficulties of raising them outside our countries.

Some months later, Martin Carnoy called me to let me know he was bringing Freire again to Stanford and asking me if I could offer him a presentation at USF. He explained Freire's difficult economic situation. Since upon his return to Brazil after many years in exile the Brazilian government was not offering him any retirement. Getting him economic help from friends abroad was important.

This presented a great problem for me. I had no resources of my own. And at that time USF had a very different attitude concerning social justice issues than today.

We were going through a period when the Board of Trustees had decided they did not like the Multicultural emphasis that had existed during the late 70s, but wanted to "white out a campus that had been built to educate the Italian and Irish youth" as a heard one of the trustees said.

Freire was considered by the administration of the time a problematic "revolutionary" and I had been told that it was not appropriate to use his theories in dissertations, although I continued to teach his work in my classes.

My only possibility was finding the resources on my own. I conceived the idea of offering a number of seminars (not for credit) for which people attending would pay a fee. The major enticement was that at the end of the seminars they would get to participate in a lecture by Freire.

Since Freire's presence in Northern California had been minimal and, up to that time, reduced to very small gatherings, this attracted a great deal of attention. The generosity of a number of activist friends

209

from the Bay Area made the plan possible when they agreed to lead the seminars *ad honorem*, knowing that all the money we collected would go directly to Freire.

The four seminars lasted several weeks meeting each on a different day from Monday to Thursday. The topics varied, but all had a social justice content. A few people attended more than one seminar, but in most cases each person attended one. This meant somewhere between 120 to 140 people.

Concurrently, I announced to my students that they would get to spend a full afternoon with Freire and listen to his evening lecture.

All I asked from the university was a room for the seminars and the use of the Lone Mountain auditorium for the evening lecture. Freire then, joined us for an afternoon with my students, and was delighted to see their dedication and commitment.

During the evening lecture the Lone Mountain Auditorium was completely full, and although Paulo had stated many times that he did not want to do public speaking to large audiences, and had agreed to do this one reluctantly, he was delighted by the questions posed to him by the audience which let him know the sincerity of the activists present.

After this I was able to have Paulo Freire several times at USF. For future visits I would propose to teach an extra course, to be attended by the doctoral students who had Title VII fellowships, as well as any other student interested, and instead of collecting what the university would have paid me for that extra work have that amount be given to Freire.

I was delighted to take the extra work for free in exchange for the privilege of having Freire present on campus.

Many of the 159 dissertations I directed used Freire's work, either as part of the Theoretical Framework, as the support for

211

their Participatory Research Methodology, or both.

Freire became very significant to the International Multicultural Program. And the university attitude towards Freire slowly changed. So that when a new faculty was selected the position was given to Father Denis Collins who had written a book on Freire.

I continued being in touch with Freire. He was kind enough to insist I would travel to Brazil so that we could record a book. By that time his first wife, Elsa, had died and he had married Nita, the extraordinary companion of his last years.

Since my arrival coincided with his previously unannounced appointment as Sao Paolo Secretary of Education, he was absorbed by responsibilities. Yet he made the time for us to do some recordings with his daughter Madalena and to make a video on Participatory Research especially for my students. This video can be seen at YouTube if one search Alma Flor Ada and Paulo Freire:

https://www.youtube.com/results?search_query=Alma+Flor+Ada+and+Paulo+Freire

I will be delighted to send a copy, as a gift, to anyone who write me requesting it: almaflor@almaflorada.com

Paulo also graciously created some precious quiet time to share with him and Nita.

A surprising anecdote
On a teaching Saturday when I walked into Lone Mountain there were signs all over inviting to listen to Freire in a given classroom, with foot prints cut outs on the floor and walls showing the way. I was most amazed by the news because I could not believe Freire would be in Lone Mountain unknown to me.

While we had created the opportunity to have Paulo at the University on several occasions, this was not one of them and I could not understand what was going on when large numbers of students, many of them not registered for the course, filled our classroom.

Once the group quieted down, with many students having to leave at the request of their somewhat annoyed professors, one of my students introduced an interview session with Paulo Freire.

Indeed, we were to hear Paulo's voice that morning. It was coming as precise responses to questions aptly posted by one of the students. But the Paulo Freire that faced us was not my beloved mentor, but a masterful creation by Julia Marshall, a doctoral student who taught art at San Francisco State University.

It took us a moment to realize how, very brilliant students had search through Paulo's recording for interesting segments and then had constructed the very appropriate questions those segments could answer.

The doctoral students who came first with the idea was Guadalupe Solís. Their group was following my request that their group

214

presentations would be both scholarly and original, not the mere reading of a paper.

The puppet is housed today, in the Paulo Freire Archives at *Chapman University* together with many of the dissertations I directed and recordings of some of the lectures Freire's gave at USF. They also have a permanent collection of my books and publications, just as eight other universities: *Fresno State University*, has predominantly my children's literature books, and those co-authored with Isabel Campoy, as well pertinent correspondence and originals in the Arne Nixon Children's Literature Center; the *University of Miami* has a permanent collection of all my publications both for children and adults in the Cuban Heritage Center; as do the *University of Georgia*, the *University of Texas at San Antonio*. Isabel and I donated a collection to *Columbia Teacher's College*, dedicated to the memory of our friend María Torres Guzmán and *Florida Southwestern State College* will receive one dedicated to the memory of our friend Lee Bennett Hopkins.

Kent State University in Ohio is developing a very large archive of my books, papers, awards, memorabilia. They are also filming a series of videos about my work and that of Isabel Campoy, with whom I have co-authored extensively, since they would like to be repositories of our lives and for that purpose has created a multidisciplinary project involving students from several disciplines.

[An update of universities and institutions holding permanent collections of my publications, as well as those of Isabel Campoy, can be seen on pages 246 and 247.]

Needless to say, should the USF Library were to express a desire to hold my books on a permanent collection, I would make all efforts to donate as complete a collection as possible.

2. What was it like working with some of the initial students like Peter Baird to establish this scholarship in Paulo Freire's honor?

Peter Baird, as many of the doctoral students I advised, was a recipient of a federal fellowship under the Title VII Bilingual Education Office. I had both recruited and advised Peter throughout the doctoral program as I did with multiple other students.

These students became a very close-knit community. Twice a year we held retreats, outside of USF, during one of the first non-teaching weekends of the semester. This allowed for ample time for dialogue, for advisement and for the development of mentorships between students that were finishing, or who had already finished the doctorate, and first year students or even prospective students.

When I announced that I would be retiring in a year several of the students talked about starting a scholarship in my name. They felt they had received much during their doctoral studies, and those who had studied through a fellowship felt compelled to give back. When I heard about it, I thank them for their willingness to give back, but asked them to reconsider creating the scholarship on Paulo Freire's name, since he had meant so much to all of us.

Personally, I had always wanted to acknowledge Paulo's contribution and collaborated in proposing him for the Nobel Prize, although he never received that recognition he so rightly deserved.

The USF scholarship would be a humbler, but very sincere, way of acknowledging the value of his work.

Peter Baird took the responsibility to talk to students about contributing. Unfortunately, once I retired and the students who had originally contributed had graduated the process became dormant, since we had not achieved the monetary goal set up by USF. We owe to Dr. Susan Katz that the dream of honoring Freire, while offering some support to deserving students, would not languish. She never gave up and finally, during the 40th anniversary of the institution of the International Multicultural Program, those attending the celebration contributed the amount needed for the scholarship to become a reality.

3. How does it feel now, as former faculty and founder of the IME department to see this scholarship finally get endowed and distributed after all these years?

I would like to clarify that the IME Program was founded by Dr. José Llanes. I joined IME on its second year, the first of the doctoral program. On the IME's third year I was given responsibility for the implementation of the doctoral program, since Dr. Llanes had left. From then onwards I was a faculty member and eventually I became responsible for the Title VII doctoral fellowship program.

All along I was very much invested in the possibilities that the IME Program offered to students of multiple origins, who having had a career in education, now wished to attain a doctorate. I was particularly interested in facilitating that deserving students would obtain the credentials that would allow them to open doors for other.

A large number of our doctoral students were first in their family to graduate from college, others even first in their families to complete a high school diploma, many were farm workers and immigrants. In most instances they were highly determined to struggle for social justice.

I am delighted to see the overall change in USF for a commitment to social justice at the whole institution and equally delighted to meet the young, bright and committed new faculty at the IME and Teacher Education Programs. It feels as if seeds planted long ago have grown unto strong blooming trees.

It is a joy that the students desire to honor Freire and support new students has finally become a reality. I trust you will share this news with Nita Freire who has, along the years, asked about the scholarship development.

4. What does it mean to you, as former faculty, to give back to USF and specifically IME students in the School of Education?

USF gave me the opportunity to work with extraordinary students, learning alongside them has been a most valuable experience, one I will always be treasured. During my long years at USF I tried to give the most and the best of me.

Now I guess all I have to give is gratitude to all the faculty and students who continue to enjoy the venue offered by USF not only for their personal growth but for that of others.

5. What are your hopes for the future of this scholarship and for future IME students who may receive it?

Now that the scholarship is fully endowed, I trust it will be given each year to a deserving student. And hope that the recipients will learn about Paulo Freire and find ways to continue his teachings. And for all students at the School of Education, and their faculty, I wish that the generous profession they have chosen, while not sufficiently recognized by society, will be for them a source of great satisfaction by learning alongside students as inspiring as the ones I was privileged to have in my classes.

Alma Flor Ada
Professor Emerita
University of San Francisco
San Rafael, CA
April 5, 2018

221

Oh, Paulo Freire, was a revolutionary
Song by Peter Baird

[tune: "O canoero" Caeyme-Brazil, lyrics- Peter Baird
©.2003 CABE, & 2015 USFIME & Scholarship]

Chorus:

> *Oh, Paulo Freire was a*
> *revolutionary Brazilian,*
> *Paulo Freire is a teacher today.*
> *Oh, Paulo Freire was a*
> *revolutionary Brazilian,*
> *Paulo Freire is a teacher today.*

When we teach about justice,
When we teach about love,
Paulo Freire is alive today. [*repeat*]
Chorus
When students learn to read,
And they read the world,
Paulo Freire is alive today. [*repeat*]
Chorus
When we challenge the system,
When we challenge ourselves,
Paulo Freire is alive today. [*repeat*]
Chorus
When we come together,
Join our voices ever,
Paulo Freire is alive today. [*repeat*]
Chorus

16.In Conclusion

Sitting at the computer to write this book, I have frequently paused to look out of my office window and admire the roses growing on my back yard, the beauty of the birds on my birdfeeders. How extraordinary their natural perfection. How different their existence of *being* from our constant efforts of *becoming*... At an earlier point in my life I thought I would have wanted my life to be one of quiet solitude... Fay Luis de León verses from the Ode *Vida retirada* called to me:

¡Qué descansada vida
la del que huye del mundanal rüido,
y sigue la escondida senda
por donde han ido
los pocos sabios que en el mundo han sido!

With apologies to Fray Luis for the poor translation: *What a restful life /the one of those*

223

who run away from the noise of the world / and choose the hidden path / followed by those few who have been truly wise.

But alas, I followed the words of another great poet, César Vallejo, who in *Poemas humanos* [1939] after reminding us:

> *Y, desgraciadamente,*
> *el dolor crece en el mundo a cada rato,*
> *crece a treinta minutos por segundo,*
> *paso a paso...*
> [And, unfortunately,
> Pain grows in the world at every moment
> It grows at thirty minutes in each second,
> Step by step...]

He claimed:

> *¡Ah, desgraciadamente, hombres humanos,*
> *hay, hermanos, muchísimo que hacer.*
> [Ah, unfortunately, human beings,
> There is, brothers and sisters, very much to be done!]

In this book I have sought to briefly describe some of the principles and practices I have developed over a lifetime of learning alongside my students who have continuously informed, challenged, and inspired me with their authenticity, their commitment, their dedication, and their hope.

One recurring thread in our work together has been the theme of gratefulness. My students and I have often reflected on the privilege implied by being able to sit and dialogue, to read and write, while so many human beings are struggling to obtain enough food to stay alive, clean water to drink, or a place to rest. I believe that this recognition of our privilege strengthened our sense of responsibility, yet it did not diminish the joy that we found in our work together.

I cannot remember a teaching weekend at the University of San Francisco in which I would be untouched by a sense of anticipation and wonder. I knew that each time, I would emerge at the end of a very intense couple of days, filled with a wealth of experiences, reflections, and ideas, enriched by the experience of having connected deeply with others, of having truly lived that which Freire used to describe as "the Joooooooy of Learning",

225

drawing out the words to emphasize how fully he savored the experience...

This was a learning so active and alive that it could never be contained within the pages of a book; instead, it was being born and evolving with each word, through each pause, in each moment of silence, in the courage of speaking our truth, acknowledging our doubts and our uncertainties, recognizing our limitations... in each moment of determining to nonetheless continue on, in the unending journey toward realizing our ideals of freedom, well-being, and justice for all —an unreachable goal maybe, yet certainly one that allows us to tap into the limitless energy of our deepest convictions.

I will always be grateful to you, my students, for what we were able to create together. May your own journeys be filled with the joy of on-going discovery, as you carry on with the larger work of teaching, learning, and growing.

This gratitude extends to everyone who during presentations, workshops, brief courses, in-service trainings, school visits, or sometimes in casual encounters, have shared with me the richness of their experiences as teachers or students renewing my hope and my belief in the power of education.

Titles of doctoral dissertations directed by Alma Flor Ada Ph.D.

International Multicultural Program
1979 - 2005
School of Education
University of San Francisco

The educators whose names are listed along their dissertation titles, honored me by requesting that I direct their dissertation.

Each one taught me about their topic and the research process, but above all they taught me about endurance and persistency, about having dreams for a better future and being willing to work for attaining it. Their social responsibility, their generosity and their determination to honor their values and their families have been a constant inspiration for me.

Alexander, Deborah Mazie. *Broken Bread and Poured Out Wine: An Ethnographic Interview Study of the Life Stories of African Ancestry Women Pastors.* 2003.

Al-Mouhandis, Zakia. *Higher Education for Women in Saudi Arabia.* 1986.

Anaya, Alfonso R. *Empowering Immigrant Migrant Mexican Parents: A Participatory Study Through Dialogic Retrospection.* 1995.

Arce, Josephine. *Developing Voices: Transformative Education in a First Grade Spanish Two-way Immersion Classroom: A Participatory Study.* 1997.

Artiga, Antonio A. *Descriptive Study on Patterns of Completion and Attrition at the Multicultural Education Doctoral Program, University of San Francisco.* 1983.

Asfoor, Majid Ahmad. *Difficulty English Speakers Encounter in Arabic Phonology.* 1982.

Ayala, Armando Alfonso. *A Comparative Analysis of the 1974 Bilingual Education Act with the Recommended Changes by Field Practitioners and the Final 1978 Bilingual Education Act.* 1983.

Baird, Peter J. *Children's Song-Makers as Messengers of Hope: Participatory Research with Implications for Teacher Educators.* 2001.

Balderas, Ricardo. *Home Language Use and the Attitudes of Bilingual Hispanic Parents and Their Spouses and the Bilingual Development of Their Children.* 1988.

Balderas, Valerie. *Reclaiming and Affirming Voice and Culture Family Contributions Through Book Creation of Lived History and Experience: A Participatory Study with Mexican Families.* 1993

Bayer, David. *The Culture of Technology or Cultural Diversity: A Survey of the Educational Philosophies of California School Principals.* 1982

Bayless, Patricia. *Teacher's Critical Reflections on Cross Cultural Understanding Through Participatory Research.* 1991.

Beihl, Barbara Pereida. *Female Elders as Culture Bearer in Multicultural Children's Literature.* 1998

Benedict, Jennifer N. *Grandparents' Images in Children's Books: Authors Reflections on Grandparent Influences: A Participatory Study.* 2001.

Berta-Avila, Margie I. *"The Cure is in the Pain" The Pedagogy of Critical Xicana/Xicano Educators in the Classroom.* 2004

Beutel, Constance. *An Examination of Transformative Education and Its Application in Pacific Bell.* 1989.

Bissember, Roy A. *Comparative School Experiences and Values of Mexican-American High School Dropouts and Graduates.* 1981.

Borunda, Rose M. *Voices from the Second Generation: Five Young Women of Mexican Descent in American School: Defining and Preserving Self/Sustaining Hope.* 2002.

Brown, Kristin. *Teacher-Researchers' Critical Reflections on the Process of Engaging in Binational Participatory Research with Puerto Rican Circular Migrant Studies.*1995.

Brown, Pamela Ann. *Young Mothers' Voices: Reflections on Abusive Relationships. A Feminist Participatory Research.* 1993.

Bryant, Dorothy E. *The Impact of Language and Culture on Medical Care.* 1999.

Campa, María Teresa. *The Transfer of Spanish Literacy to English Reading: A Participatory Study with Effective Elementary Level Bilingual Teachers.* 1993.

Ceballos, Pansy. *The Manifestation of Voice and Language in Spanish Speaking Second Language Learners. A Participatory Study.* 1998.

Chisholm, Maia Joan. *Post-Secondary Vocational Education: A Participatory Study of the Contributing*

Factors that Lead to Mexican-American Women's Self-Actualization in the Workplace. 2002.

Cho, Eun Mi. *The Role of Communication in Providing Effective Special Education Services for Korean-American Children with Specific Learning Disabilities: A Participatory Study.* 1998.

Choy, Valkyrie Kanani. *Parents' Critical Reflections on an Elementary Japanese Bilingual Bicultural Public-School Program: A Participatory Research Study.* 1993.

Cohen, Sam W. *The Sequential Order of Acquisition of Spanish Verb Tenses among Spanish-Speaking Children, Ages 3-7.* 1980.

Contreras, Marcos. *Hispanic Graduates of Higher Education: A Critical Reflection of Their Experience.* 1993.

Cordova, Carlos B. *Migration and Acculturation Processes of Undocumented El Salvadorans in the San Francisco Bay Area.* 1986.

Davis, Charlotte M. *Towards Empowerment of Youth: A Participatory Study of a Summer Employment Program.* 1985.

Del Portillo, Raymond. *The Relationship between an Elementary Principal's Behavior and the Quality of the Spanish Bilingual Program in the School.* 1989.

DellaMaggiore, Glenn. *Bilingual Education: A Comparison of Academic Achievement in Bilingual vs. Monolingual Classrooms.* 1989.

Devich, Heather. *School Education as a Tool for Social Change: Study of an Arizona Inner City Charter School.* 2000.

Di Stefano, Rachelle. *From School to Career: A Participatory Study of Urban African American Realities.* 1998.

Díaz, Richard. *The Education of Chicano Students, Parents and Teachers at the Calmecac Leadership Institute: A Participatory Study.* 1998.

Díaz-Greenberg, Rosario. *Freire's Liberatory Education: The Emergence of Voice in Latin High School Students Through Participatory Research.* 1995.

Dolson, David. *The Influence of Various Home Bilingual Environments on the Academic Achievement Language Development and Psycho-Social Adjustment of Fifth and Sixth Grade Hispanic Students.* 1981.

Domínguez, Enrique O. *Heritage Language as Portrayed in Literature Written by Latino Authors: A Transformative Critical Literary Approach.* 2004.

Dresser, Rocío. *Teaching Metacognitive Strategies to English Language Learners in the Upper Elementary Grades: A Participatory Study with Bilingual Teachers.* 2000.

Duffala, Joyce. *The Rittenberg/Kreitzer Theater-Based "Active Communicating" Process and Interpersonal Communication in the Corporation: A Participatory Study*. 1992.

El-Barouki, Foazi. *A Culturally Based Analysis of Selected Idiomatic Expressions in Arabic*. 1985.

Emanuel, Itzhak. *The Bureau of Jewish Education of San Francisco, Marin County and the Peninsula in the State of California: The Effectiveness of Implementation of Goals, 1977-1982*. 1983.

Espinosa-Álvarez, María. *Mexican Working Mothers and Their Family Legacy: A Participatory Research Study*. 1999.

Espinoza, Frank. *Language Loss and Its Impact on the Self-Concept of Monolingual English-Speaking Hispanics: A Participatory Research*. 1996.

Estrada, Jorge. *A Study of How Hispanics Are Depicted in the California State-Adopted Sixth Grade Reading Texts in 1982*. 1987.

Fernandez, Gloria. *Using LEGO/LOGO in the Primary Classroom: A Case Study*. 1993.

Gallardo, Olivia. *Creating Linguistic Equity: An Empowerment Model for Teachers, Parents and Students in a Kindergarten Classroom. A Participatory/Action Research*. 1999.

García-Canales, Carmen. *Noun Repertoire of Spanish Pre-Kindergarten Age Children Compared with Kindergarten Teachers' Expectation.*1981.

Gelardin, Sally D. *Life Transitions & Lifework Success: The Influence of Mother-Daughter Relationships Among Women of Eastern European Jewish Descent.* 1999.

Genera, Evangelina. *Chicano Students' Responses to Community College Academic Enrichment Programs: Critical Reflections of Their Educational Experiences. A Participatory Study.* 1993.

Glugoski, Greta. *A Study of the Self Concepts of Elderly Hispanic Women: Las Ancianas.* 1989.

Gómez, Inés. *Disruption and Relocation: Chilean Women in Exile, a Participatory Research Study.* 1993.

Gómez-Montejano, *Sarah. CBEST the Gatekeeper: A Participatory Study about the Use and Effects of the Basics Skills Exams in the Teaching Professions.* 1993.

Gómez-Valdez, Cristina. *The Silent Majority Raise Their Voices: Reflections of Mexican Parents on Learning and Schooling: A Participatory Research.* 1993.

Gonzalez, Jacob E. *An Analysis of Successful Hispanic Immigrants in the San Francisco Bay Area.* 1989.

Graziano, Kevin. *Through Their Own Eyes: A Photovoice and Participatory Analysis into the Lives of Black Gay and Lesbian South Africans.* 2003.

Griffin, Gregory. *Community and Crisis in a Rural Community: A Cultural Transition.* 1996.

Guerrero, Marcos P. *Spanish-Speaking Students' Critical Analysis of Their Educational Experiences: A Participatory Study.* 1989.

Hale, Aileen W. *Second Language Acquisition and Cultural Understanding through Service-learning in Higher Education: A Participatory Research.* 1997.

Halpin, Marianne. *Naming Ourselves: A Participatory Research with Hapa Authors of Japanese Ancestry Writing for Children or Young Adults.* 2003.

Heathcote, Olivia D. *The Sex Stereotypes Present in Mexican Reading Primers Published in 1960 and those Published in 1972.* 1980.

Hernández, Rosa G. *The Influence of Mothers on the Educational Attainment of Second-Generation Latina Professional Daughters of Farm Working Family Backgrounds: A Participatory Research Study.* 2001

Hock, Beverly Vaughn. *The Labyrinth of Story: Narrative as Creative Connection.* 1999.

Howard, Katsuyo. *Practices and Reflection on Parenting Among College-Educated Parents: A Participatory Research*. 1996.

Hubler, Sandra J. *Voices of Chinese American Women: The Arduous Pursuit of a College Education. A Participatory Research*. 1998.

Huertas, Cristina V. *A Spanish Auditory Comprehension Language Test: Development and Validation*. 1989.

Hurtado, Rosemary. *The Bilingual Reading Process of Adult Spanish Speakers Reading English as a Second Language*. 1985.

Igoa, Cristina. *Toward a Psychology and Education of the Oppressed: A Study of the Inner World of Immigrant Children*. 1988.

Isola, Raymond. *The Influence of Participatory Professional Development Experiences on the Formation of Teacher Self-Concept: A Participatory Research Study of Elementary School Teachers*. 2001.

James, Ryan. *The Lozanov Method/Accelerated Learning and Total Immersion in Adult Second Language Learning: Teachers' Reflections on the Effectiveness of Non-Traditional Methods*. 2000.

Janssens, Luc. *The Integration of Hmong Adults into American Society through the Community College: A Participatory Study of the Possibilities of Cultural Preservation.* 1987.

Judd, Judy. *Intercultural Children's Literature: A Critical Analysis of Picture Books Published between 1983 and 1998.* 1999.

Jue, Jennifer. *Chinese American Women's Development of Voice and Cultural Identity: A Participatory Research Study via Feminist Oral History.* 1993.

Kaiser, Karen. *Latino Family Literacy Projects: Developing Home to School Connections through Children's Literature and Dialogue.* 2005.

Kanell, Rita. *Grandparents and other Elders' Role at the Turn of the Millennium: Their Portrayal in Multicultural Children's Literature.* 2000.

Keis, Richard B. *Developing Authorship in Latino Parents: A Case Study of the Libros y Familias Program.* 2002.

Kelly, Carole M. *Hispanic Cultural Values and the Education of Spanish-Speaking Students: A Literary Perspective.* 1979.

Kitchin, Deborah. *Case Study of ESL Community College Students Using Computer-Based Writing Tools in a Composition Course.* 1991.

La Torre, Evelyn. *School Identification Profile and Child-Family Interaction Frequency of Non-Communicatively Handicapped Four to Six-Year-Old Spanish Speakers.* 1982.

Lango, Deborah. *Mexican American Women who Transfer from a Community College to a Four-Year University: Participatory Research on Persistence.* 1998.

LaTorre-Derby, Jan. *Towards a Transformative Classroom: A Critical Analysis of School Partnerships in a Multicultural Setting.* 1993.

Laughlin, Margaret. *Crossing Borders: Transformative Experiences of Euro American Bilingual Teachers in a Spanish Speaking Context: A Participatory Study.* 1996.

LeBeouf, Cheryl. *The Education Experience of Newly-Arrived Immigrant High School Students: A Participatory Reflection.* 1990.

Lipman, David. *Oppression, Liberation, and Language: A Participatory Study of Gay Bilinguals.* 2003.

Lobo, Charlene P. *Telling It Like It Is: Disempowerment and Marginalization of First-Generation, Low-Income College Students: A Participatory Research.* 2001.

Lopez, Martha. *Critical Pedagogy for Hispanic Consumers: A Participatory Exploration of Hispanic Women's Reflections on Marketing Practices*. 1998.

Low, Victor. *The Chinese in the San Francisco Public School System: A Historical Study of One Minority Group Response to Educational Discrimination, 1859-1959*.1981.

Lowenthal, Marla. *The Internationalization of Higher Education*. 1998.

Luna, Debra A. *When "Inclusion" Means Exclusion: A Participatory Research Journey into the Educational Experiences of First and Second-Generation Mexican Immigrant Females and their Parents' Reflections*. 2002.

Lynn, Charlie R. *The De(con)struction of Butch and Nelly: Participatory Research Regarding Gender Identity and Gender Self-Concept of Gay Men*. 2001.

Mackeben, Daniel Clark. *International Student Reflections on Issues of Discrimination at U.S. Colleges and Universities*. 1999.

Marshall, Julia. *Making Meaning: Transformative Art Education for Middle School*. 1998.

Martínez, María Norma. *The Principal's Role in Promoting Success for Culturally and Linguistically Diverse Students: A Participatory Research Study.* 2003.

Mata-Palacio, María. *Emergence of a Hispanic Oasis in Children's Literature in the United States.* 1993.

Matsubayashi, Yoshihide. *The Japanese Language Schools in Hawaii and California from 1892 to 1941.* 1984.

Mayer, Jan. *The Empowerment of Ethnolinguistic Minority Students through an Interactive Pedagogy within an Additive Bilingual Environment.* 1988.

McCaleb, Sudia Paloma. *Parent Involvement in Education during Early Literacy Development: A Participatory Study with Hispanic, African American and African Parents through Dialogue and Co-Authorship of Books.* 1992.

McCall-Pérez, Zaida. *The Latina Adolescent Experience: Participatory Research: Listening to Voices in a Newcomer Center.* 1991.

Michel, José Roberto. *Access and Engagement at the Community College: Program Design and Instructional Approaches. A Participatory Study with Immigrant Mexican Women Learners and their Instructors.* 2002.

Miller, Robert. *Public Primary School Education in Mexico: A Focus on Reading Instruction in Mexico City*.1980.

Mixon, Myrtis. *Cajun Values: Identity Markers of the Louisiana Bayou Culture in Cajun Folktales*. 2000.

Montiel, Reyes. *Implementation and Evaluation of a PSI Mastery-Based Curriculum in General Studies for the "Colegio Universitario de Cabimas," Venezuela*. 1980.

Morales, Marta. *From Despair to Hope: Immigrant Families' Journey through Parent Education and Parent Involvement*. 2004.

Morales, Rosario. *Life and Reflections of Mexican and Mexican-American Traditional Storytellers: A Participatory Research*. 1993.

Moreno, Barbara. *Empowering Young Children to Think and Act Critically through Folktales: An Experience in Critical Thinking*. 1990.

Morris, Estella. *Determining Successful Bilingual Paraprofessional Inservice Training Program Characteristics: An In-Depth Study of Three Training Approaches*. 1981.

Morrison, Richard. *Another Trail of Tears: Native American Access to Higher Education Action Research*. 1998

Murillo, Salvador. *Towards Improved Home-School Interaction: A Participatory Dialogue with Hispanic Parents in Berkeley, California.* 1987

Naser, Sami. *The Impact of the American Culture on Male Arab Students in the United States.* 1984.
Niepoth, Marilyn. *The Use of Participatory Methods to Plan Educational Experiences for Students Learning English as a Second Language.* 1992.

Nim, Naomi. *Discourse of an Emerging Culture, inter-Group Community among Young Adult Friends, Israeli Jews and Palestinian Israeli Arabs.* 1988.

Norris, Aine J. Kyne. *The Unheard Voices of Turtle Island: Native American Authors of Children's Literature in the United States.* 1998.

Oladele, Folasade. *Spirit: A Missing Link in the Conception of the Education of African American Students.* 1999.

Olson, Christine Zohar. *Croatian-American Ethnic Identity Retention through Cultural Expression as Perceived within a Socio-Political Context: A Participatory Research.* 1998.

Orta-Camilleri, Emerita. *Shattering the Glass Ceiling: Critical Reflections of Latina Educational Site Administrators and What Influenced Their Success: A Participatory Study.* 1999.

Pak, Nomyon. *Korean American Acculturation Level, Value System and Attitudes towards Bilingual Education in Northern California.* 1984.

Parra, Rosa M. de Lourdes. *The Sequential Order of Acquisition of Categories of Spanish Adjectives by Spanish-Speaking Children, Ages 2 to 12 Years.* 1982.

Patrón, Rose Lee. *Promoting English Literacy for Spanish-Speaking Students: A Participatory Study of Spanish-Speaking Parents, their Children and School Personnel, Using an Innovative Intervention Model in Spanish.* 1986.

Persiani, Kimberly A. *Empowering Third Grade Children to Reflect and Respond Critically Through the Use of Multicultural Children's Literature: A Participatory Study.* 2003.

Pisano-Pugh, Gabriela. *Bilingual Bicultural Education at the California Community College: A Descriptive Study of Spanish-English Programs.* 1979.

Pitot, Mary Michelle. *Invisible and Ignored or Out and Pushed Out: Participatory Research with Gay and Lesbian Youth.* 1996.

Quevedo, Aurora Martínez. *Integrity of Culture in Professional Latina Women: The Role of Culture and Intuition in the Personal and Professional Experiences of Bilingual Latinas.* 1999.

Ramírez, Celia Acuña. *Education of Latino Migrant High School Students: Critical Reflections of Students, Counselors, and Teachers. A Participatory Study.* 1999.

Ramírez, Jorge A. *Critical Reflections of Latino Parents Regarding Opression in the Educational System and Native Language and Culture Maintenance and Loss.* 2002.

Reichmuth, Stella. *Hispanic Parent Empowerment through Critical Dialogue and Parent-Child Interaction within the School Setting.* 1988.

Reveles, Francisco. *Adolescent Hispanic Gang Members with the Context of Their School and Community Experiences: A Participatory Study.* 1993.

Reza, Jacquelyn V. *The Voice of Latina Leadership. A Participatory Research: Leading through Our Tears.* 1995.

Ríos, Herminio C. *A Historical and Comparative Content and Linguistic Analysis of the Development of the Image of the Chicano in Literature. Its Implications to Education.* 1980.

Rittenberg, Mark. *Community Literacy Projects and the Development of Self in Black South African Townships: Reflections of the People. A Participatory Study.* 1993.

Rodríguez, Annie Torres. *Shattered Relationships: The emotional Effect of Prison Life on Chicana Women and their Children*.2000.

Ruumet, Marika. *Values in the Best-Selling Children's Books in the United States, 1990-1997.* 1998.

Samuelson, Rami. *The Mizo People: Cultural Analysis of Life in a Mizo Village in the 1890s.* 1990.

Scroggins, Carol. *Women and Illiteracy: A Dialogic Investigation.* 1988.

Shaw, Carol. *Quench Not the Spirit - Young Voices Reflect on High School: A Participatory Research.* 1993.

Silva, Duarte. *Critical Reflection: Its Role in Professional Development Programs for Practicing Educators. A Participatory Research with Language Teachers.* 1993.

Smith, Jerilynn. *The Fontana Bilingual Teacher Career Ladder Program: A Participatory Study.* 1993.

Smith, Kweku Mensah. *Kwame Nkrumah: Philosophy of Education for Ghana, Africa from 1951 to 1996: An Exposition of His Life, Work and Thoughts.* 2000

Smith, Nancy J. *Linguistic Genocide and the Struggle for Cultural and Linguistic Survival: A Participatory Research Study with a Zapotec Community in California.* 1995.

Solís, Guadalupe. *Critical Reflections of Hispanic Bilingual Teachers who were former Bilingual Education Students: A Participatory Study.* 1997.

Souza, Steven. *A Decade of Institutional Discrimination in a School District: A Participatory Study.* 1992.

Spencer, Marc Harold. *Urban Youth's Critical Reflections: Indicators of Quality in Upward bound Programs.* 2005.

Suzara, Nina Macasaet. *A Spiritual Model of Acculturation: An Active Contextualized Learning Process in the Practice and Valuing of Unity in Diversity.* 1998.

Tankersley, Dawn. *Language as Resource for Peace: Critical Reflections on Bridging Two Cultures in a Dual Language Immersion Program in Macedonia.* 1999.

Tarango, Isidro. *The California Mini Corps: A Historical Study.* 1987.

Tominaga, Yasuhiko. *Dialect Comprehensibility in Japan: A Study in Determining the Linguistic Distance between Dialects of the Japanese Language.* 1988.

247

Torrey, María V. *Puerto Rican Authors: Voicing Identity in Puerto Rican Literature.* 2003.

Trujillo, Lorenzo. *The Effects of a Hispanic Ethnic Dance Curriculum upon High School Students' Self-Concept and Academic Performance.* 1979.

Valenzuela-Smith, Marina. *The Effects of a Tutorial Program for Junior High School Latino Students.* 1984.

Varisco de García, Norma. *Hispanic Women: Portraits of Leadership.* 1990.

Varona, Lucía. *How Cultural Stereotypes Affect Hispanic Women College Students: A Participatory Research.* 1996.

Watts, Joyce. *A Determination of Parental Expectations and Role in the Educational Process: Perspectives of African-American Parents.* 1988.

Willey, Sharon. *Expanding Racial Consciousness: A Participatory Study Exploring White College Administrators' Understanding of Whiteness and Racism.* 2002.

Wilson, Carol. *Women and Illiteracy: A Dialogic Investigation.* 1988.

Winkley, Cheryl. *Teachers Perspectives on Authorship as a Pedagogical Tool to Develop Voice: A Participatory Study.* 2005.

Wood, Santiago. *International Business Education Programs in the California Community Colleges.* 1986.

Worlund, Sylvia. *Attitudes of Soviet-Jewish Patients toward American Healthcare Contrasted with American Healthcare Professionals' Perceptions of Those Attitudes.* 1986.

Wu, Rina. *Experiences and Reflections of Chinese Immigrant Youth: Implications for Education. A Participatory Research.* 1990.

Yau, Rittchell Ann. *The Portrayal of Immigration in a Selection of Picture Books Published Since 1970.* 2003.

Young, Janice Ling. *The Subject of Disability in Children's Literature in the United States: A Critical Literary Analysis of Picture Books and Young Readers' Novels.* 2005.

Gratitude

Family

As I get to the final reflections it becomes evident that my most prevalent feeling along my life has been that of gratitude. As I try to visualize how to recognize those who have made my life so rewarding, it seems that perhaps I should write a book just to acknowledge them all, and perhaps I still will. Meanwhile, this book will recognize some of them, grouping them by place, time, or experience. Unquestionably some would deserve to be included in many categories. I trust that even if they find their name only in one, they will recognize my gratitude extends to their presence in many other capacities

First, once more, I recognize my pedagogical heritage and thank my great-grandparents: Lorenzo Lafuente Garoña y Virginia Rubio Sierra, educators in Madrid, and my great- grandfather Federico Salvador Arias, a man of vision who chose that his daughters be educated by María Luisa Dolz, feminist and progressive educator, whose influence was passed on from my grandmother to her daughters.

My gratitude goes also to my grandparents, Medardo Lafuente Rubio and Dolores Salvador Mendez, who educated as teachers, authors and speakers. To my grandfather Modesto Ada Barral who educated through his newspaper and his radio station.

My parents were teachers as much in everyday living as in their classrooms, a trait shared by my aunts Virginia, Mireya and Lolita Lafuente Salvador.

My uncle Mario Ada Rey was a rural teacher and from him I learned the difficult conditions of rural schools in Cuba in the 1950s. When I saw him in 1980, after 20 years, he had become a teacher educator. My uncle Manuel Ada Rey, a physician, wrote me extensive letters reaffirming the value I see in that form of expression.

251

My uncle Manolo Díaz Estrada, was not an educator in the formal sense, but as an incomparable storyteller listening to his stories was an excellent model for me. To them all, my gratitude.

Being a member of a very large family of generous, hard-working, creative, responsible sisters, nephews and nieces, cousins and their children, who look for ways to stay close while living geographically dispersed is also something for which I am thankful.

In expressing my gratitude, my four children, Rosalma, Alfonso, Miguel, Gabriel Zubizarreta-Ada, deserve a special recognition. They taught me, as our children do, when I was being effective and when I was missing the mark. Their love, patience and forgiveness were unsurpassable and helped me become a better human being.

They have added richness to my life with their spouses, Denise Pudelski, Hannah Brooks, Denia Zamperlini and Bruce Nayowith and the promise of the future in their children Tim, Samantha, Camille, Daniel, Victoria, Cristina, Jessica, Nick and Collette Zubizarreta, Tessa and Hannah Nayowith and Marion Zamperlini.

And my family has given me twice as much joy for sharing it with Isabel Campoy as she shared with me the Campoy Coronado family.

Life Experiences

Throughout life, I have been blessed by the presence of many who, in various ways, have become my mentors. I list the following names here with deep appreciation and humility, wishing I could have been able to do more in recognition of what I received from each of them.

In Camagüey, Cuba
During my elementary school
    Gladys Carnero, *Colegio Episcopal*
    Dra. María Josefa Herrera, *Colegio Zayas*
    Dra. Rosa María Peyrellade, *Escuela Anexa a la Normal de Maestros,*
     inspiring model of a teacher.

Gilda Zaldívar Freire, remarkable ballerina and exquisite human being who invited my child spirit to dream of beauty.

During my High School years at the Instituto de Segunda Enseñanza de Camagüey
Dr. Luis Martínez
and outside of class
Dra. Lar Juárez, *for inviting me to discover beauty in art*
Drs. Jorge Castellanos and Pilarín Novel, *for enriching dialogue*
Luis Aguirre, *for helping me celebrate music and teaching me to trust my voice*
Yolanda Faggioni, *for fostering my love of reading and facilitating receiving a scholarship to Loretto Heights College,*
Marta Carbonell, *for 70 years long Invaluable friendship.*

In Loretto Heights College, Denver, CO.
The sisters of Loretto, for their spirit as educators and their commitment to social justice, specially,
Sister Concilia,
Sister Mary Frances

At the Facultad de Filología, Universidad Complutense, Madrid

Dr. Dámaso Alonso, Director, and all professors of the *Programa de Cultura Hispánica* who conferred upon me the first *Premio Extraordinario* of the program, and in particular:

> **Dra. Elena Catena de Vindell**, *for developing such an interest in me and for continuing to encourage me throughout my life*
> **Dr. José Pita Andrade**, *for an Incomparable courses in Spanish and European Art and his cordiality*
> **Dr. José Cepeda Adán** *for a highly enriching course on Spanish History and for distinguishing me with his friendship*

in Spain,

> **Alonso Zamora Vicente** y **María Josefa Canellada**, *life-long models of outstanding intellectuals, maestros, and human beings.*
> **Berta Pallares Garzón**, *for sharing her exquisite approach to life, sharing with me her love for literature and art, and her tender sisterly caring.*

At the Catholic University, Lima, Perú

Dr. Luis Jaime Cisneros, *for his passion for the Spanish language*
Gustavo Gutiérrez, *for his friendship then, and for having written* La Teología de la Liberación.
Dra. Gred Ibscher, *for her model of Scholarship, exciting Latin classes, and profound kindness*

In Perú

Dr. Augusto Salazar Bondy, *for facilitating the publication of my first books, inviting me to collaborate on his philosophy anthologies, asking me to translate pieces from English. And for opening for me a new amazing world.*
Sebastián Salazar Bondy, *for understanding my loneliness and offering his friendship.*
José María Arguedas *for depicting the Peruvian reality in such vivid terms that inspired my students and for his affection for my little Rosalma.*
Dra. Beatriz Benoit, *model of intellectual and educator, for opening for me the doors of the Colegio Alexander*

*von Humboldt, and for being the best
friend, I so sorely miss.*

**My students at the Colegios
Abraham Lincoln and Alexander
von Humboldt, beloved students
then, beloved friends today**: *the
richness of your lives today, and your
contributions to the World, fill me with
joy, that you continue to see me as your
friend renews my beliefs on
teacher/student mentorship.*

At Harvard University
during my tenure as a Radcliffe
Institute Scholar and later on:
Jorge Guillén *for his generous
reception of my study about Pedro
Salinas, facilitating that I would be
appointed scholar at Radcliffe Institute
and for later writing the preface to my
book* Pedro Salinas: El diálogo
creador.
*His generosity attest to the fact that he
was as great as a man and as a poet.*
Juan Marichal and **Solita Salinas** *for
making possible my presence, and that of
my family, in Massachusetts, and for
their constant kindness.*

Teresa Guillén and **Stephen Gillman** *for a sincere friendship towards the very young woman I was, when they were already luminaries*

Joan Alonso, *who understood my admiration for his late husband Amado Alonso, and offered me motherly tenderness*

Raimundo Lida *who allowed me to experience what an outstanding teacher and mentor is. My gratitude in my name and that of my students, if I was able to guide their research, it was because of your modeling.*

At Mercy College, Detroit, Michigan

Dr. Phyllis Noda, *for the warm Welcome which grew unto friendship and your support of my proposal for a Bilingual Teacher Training Program which you fully developed and continued… and for all the good times.*

María Torres Guzmán *for the friendship that began in the process of organizing the* Michigan Education and the Latino Conference, *for later giving me the honor of writing the preface for the book* Learning in Two

Worlds *co-authored with Bertha Pérez,*
 and for the inspiration your life
continued to be.
Sister Sugrue, *for supporting my*
interest in the Latino community and the
decision to organize the 1st Conference
of Michigan Education and the
Latino a Mercy College.
Sister Christopher. Her
responsibilities as the leader of a
college never prevented her from
 showing great kindness to my
children, who renamed her *Sister*
 Christopher Robin while enjoying the
time we spent in a college dorm and
in a Novitiate while waiting to be
 able to move into our new home.

University of San Francisco
Colleagues

Dr. José Llanes, who invited me to
join the International Multicultural
Program and **Dr. Alan Calvin** who
supported my appointment.

Dr. Susan Roberta Katz, for her generous recognition of my work during my retirement ceremony and during the celebration of the 40th anniversary of the IME Program.

My colleagues in the School of Education, particularly **Fr. Dennis Collins, Dr. Anita De Frantz, Dr. Elena Flores, Dr. Emilie Giraux,** and **Dr. Annie Herda** and the students who became my teachers and my friends.

The **Faculty Union** who supported my grievance against the University when it was necessary to obtain justice.

To all the extraordinary friends who were generously willing to accept my invitation, in most instances with no monetary remuneration, to speak to my students, and whose presence in our classrooms was such a highlight in their academic development, among them:
Jim Cummins

Henry Giroux
Stephen Krashen
Peter McClaren
Robert Phillipson
Mary Popplin
Tove Skutnabb-Kangas
María Torres Guzmán
Catherine Walsh

Students

To the doctoral students who honored me by asking me to be their dissertation advisor and enriched my academic and personal life through this interaction.

Their names are listed with the titles of their dissertations in the previous section. Some have become my friends and I treasure our continuing interacting, among them:

Alfonso Anaya, Josie Arce, Rosita Arenas, Peter Baird, Valerie Balderas, David Bayer, Jennifer Benedict, Margarita Berta-Ávila, Pansy Ceballos, Ray del Portillo David Dolson, Joyce Duffala, Itzhak Emmanuel, Sally Gelardin, Inés Gómez, Rosa Hernández, Jennifer Jue, Rita Kanell, Margaret Laughlin,

Charlene Lobo, Marla Lowenthal, Debra Luna, Julia Marshall, Gabriela Pisano, Michelle Pitot, Rose Lee Patrón, Aurora Quevedo, Celia Ramírez, Jorge Ramírez, Francisco Reveles, Mark Rittenberg, James Ryan, Carol Shaw, Duarte Silva, Jerilyn Smith, María Victoria Torrey, Joyce Watts, Cheryl Winkle.

To all those students who were willing to assume *ad honorem* the responsibility of being my Teaching Assistants, and whose contributions made our courses much more meaningful and vibrant, among them, **Constance Beutel, Kristin Brown, Folasade Odalede, Jackie Reza, Guadalupe Solís, Nancy Jean Smith, Beverly Vaughn Hock.**

The students and graduates who organized and participated in a most beautiful retirement festivity to celebrate my retirement, on August 28, 2005, at the R. L. White Retreat Center in Mill Valley, where we had enjoyed our bi-annual retreats, and who left me very generous written testimonies, artistically presented of our joint journey: **Michelle Amberg-Espinosa, Martina Ayala, Peter Baird** and his lovely and supportive wife **Joy, Jennifer Benedict, Kristin Brown, Charlotte Davies, Rocío Dresser, Susan Gold, Rebeca García González, Marianne Halpin, Tracy Hefferman, Cristina Igoa, Karen Kayser, Myrtis Mixon, Rosario Morales, Sudía Paloma McCaleb, Dulce María Pérez** and her precious little daughter **Amelia, Kimberly Persiani, Aurora Quevedo, Lettie Ramírez, Duarte Silva, Jerilyn Smith, Nancy Jean Smith, Guadalupe Solís, Cheryl Winkle.**

A very special gift was the painting done by **Rosita Arenas**, with the signatures of many of my students in the border. It hangs in front of my desk and I am watching it as I type these lines, with the same gratitude I have been watching it since I received it.

The former students who contributed chapters to the book *Multicultural Education in Practice: Transforming One Community at a Time*, so generously published in my honor: **Josephine Arce, Peter Baird, Rose Borunda, Evangelina Brignoni, Eun Mi Cho, Zaida Mc-Call Pérez**, and to the enthusiastic creators of the project and contributing editors : **Olivia M. Gallardo** and **Lettie Ramírez**.

As well as the former students who have given me the honor and joy of writing prefaces for their own books: *Building Communities of Learners. A Collaboration among Teachers, Students, Families and Communities*, by Dr. Sudía Paloma McCaleb.
Connections and Commitments. Reflecting Latino Values in Early Childhood Programs by Costanza Eggers-Piérola, who although not an IME student joined our community visiting our classes while studying her doctorate at Harvard.
The Inner World of the Immigrant Child by Dr. Cristina Igoa;

No estás solo: Recetas para obtener éxito de padres para padres edited by **Dr. Lettie Ramírez**, who although never formally an IME student joined our community of learners enriching it with her generosity and her exciting projects.

And all the enthusiastic students who participated in making the *Reading the World Conference*, such an outstanding series of events, among them:
Rosita Arenas, Jeniffer Benedict, Pansy Ceballos, Eun Mi Cho, Ellie Galvez-Hard, Sally Gelardin, Kevin Graziano, Marianne Halpin, Tracy Hefferman, Caryl Hodges, Rita Kanell, Deborah Lango, Marla Lowenthal, Julia Marshall, Myrtis Mixon, Rosario Morales, Mary Louise Newling, Joanne Norris, Melba Patillo-Beals, Kimberly Persiani, Barbara Selvidge, Jerilyn Smith, Guadalupe Solís, M. Victoria Torrey and very specially to **Dr. Beverly Vaughn Hock** whose leadership

made these amazing gatherings of authors and educators possible.

To read more about the conference: www.almaflorada.com/reading-the-world-conference/

At CABE, NABE, ILA, AERA, and other professional organizations
> To all educators who create spaces to share their commitment to facilitate intellectual and pedagogical growth. To these organizations for supporting their work, with humility for the recognition given my work.

As an author
> My gratitude goes to all the authors, in various genres, whose words have delighted, informed and challenged me from my early years until today. Their works have been constant source of inspiration.

> To the librarians and teachers who facilitate the magical encounter

between readers and books and provide a safe space in their libraries.

I am also very thankful to the universities and institutions that hold in their libraries Alma Flor Ada & Isabel Campoy Permanent Collections. They are, up to the present:

Columbia Teacher's College
   In honor of María Torres Guzmán
Florida Southwestern State College
   In honor of Lee Bennet Hopkins
Georgia State University
   In honor of Virginia de Miranda Balbona
Instituto Cervantes, New York
   In honor of the Campoy Coronado and the Ada Lafuente families
St. Thomas University, Houston
   In honor of Alma Lafuente de Ada
Spanish Consulate in Los Ángeles– Education Department
   In honor of the Campoy Coronado and the Ada Lafuente families
University of Arizona
   World of Words Center
   In honor of Pilar Campoy

University of Miami
Cuban Heritage Collection
University of Texas, San Antonio
In honor of the Campoy Coronado and the Ada Lafuente families
University of Texas, El Paso.
In honor of Alma Lafuente de Ada
The **Arne Nixon Center, at Fresno State University** archives besides the permanent collection many of our papers and artifacts.

Chapman University, holds copies of the dissertations chaired by me as well as some course materials and recordings of Paulo Freire's visits to USD in the Paulo Freire Archives.

Kent State University, Kent, Ohio, is developing an interdisciplinary archiving project which includes books authored by teachers and children, correspondence, digitalized interviews, and videos of presentations. Their intention is to be full repositories of our lives work, as educators, authors, translators, speakers, and more.

Publishers and editors, illustrators and designers, translators and proof readers, who have transformed my manuscripts in published books for children and adults all have my gratitude.

In the forthcoming book **My Books, My Life,** I share in more detail this aspect of my life and name specifically many of those who have contributed to that journey.

A special thanks

To the dear friends who read this book at different stages of creation and provided meaningful feedback:

> **Kristin Brown,**
> **Diana Campoamor,**
> **Marla Lowenthal,** and
> **John Marino.**

And to my former students, always my friends and teachers:

> **Beverly Vaughn Hock,**
> **Jackie Reza** and
> **Nancy Jean Smith**

for their invaluable collaboration on Chapters 12, 13 and 14.

And always, everywhere
My profound gratitude to
Paulo Freire and **Nita Araujo Freire**
whose teaching I try to follow.

Appendixes

To create an "I Am" poem

1. PERSONAL "I AM" BOOK

➤ Metaphoric "I Am" book
Begin each verse with the statement "I am" and complete it presenting yourself in terms of:

- colors, fragrances, feelings, food, music, song.
- As a part of nature: ocean, mountains, desert, fields, trees or flowers, animals, birds, fish.
- As a place or object in your house, an element of your life.
- As a culture icon
- As any image that represents you.

➤ Relationship "I Am" book
Present yourself as member of a relationship, in terms of daughter/son; sister/brother; aunt/uncle/ friend, mentor, neighbor, etc.

➤ Acrostic "I Am" book
Use each letter of your name to guide the structure of the book

➤ Combination or Original structure "I Am" book
Dare to be creative:
the sky is the limit.

2. INVITE THE CLASS TO CREATIVE A COLLECTIVE POEM "I AM"

Create a collective poem by having each student provide an "I am" metaphoric line.

3. CREATE A CLASS BOOK

Include your poem, the students' collective poem, and their individual poems.

In some instances, my doctoral students were willing to include individual photographs with their poems, to take collective photographs, or even dared to create pieces of art to accompany their poems.

These poems, shared with the class, contribute to create a better understanding of each person and of the community of learners.

To create a "Where I Come From" Poem

The process is best begun by sharing a "Where I Come From", either one previously chosen or created by you. There are many available in www.authorsintheclassroom.com The following can also be shared:

Where I Come From
F. Isabel Campoy

I come from a street that leads to the desert
        and from a house with balconies
facing the sea.
I come from clothes drying under the sun,
        and the smell of soap, of Mondays, of
        work.
I come from María and Diego,
        peasants and poets, laborers of love.
I come from jumping rope and playing
        marbles, molding mud into cups and
        sauces, building castles in the sand.
I come from rice and fried chicken,
        watermelon, tortillas y pan.
I come from poverty and hard work,
        from honor and pride.

I come from a country, Spain, that lost a
    war against itself and suffered 36
    years of crime, of silence, of shame.
I come from the certainty of giving voice to
    our hearts so that together we create
    new days of peace.
Full of compassion,
    full or pride and pain,
    I say:
        This is where I come from.

I. CREATE A WHERE I COME FROM POEM OR BOOK.

These steps can be useful, but do not feel limited by them. Feel free to begin each sentence with the words: "I come from" or "Where I'm from".

1. Imagine yourself at a specific age in childhood: 7, 8, 9, 12 years old
2. List some of the most memorable items you see in your childhood home.
3. Step outside. List what you see around you: in the front yard, the backyard, the street, the neighborhood.
4. State the names of relatives or caretakers, those who link you to your past.
5. Write down frequently heard words, sayings or expressions. Which sentences that you heard over and over would distinguish your family from others?

6. Name food and dishes from family gatherings, daily meals or special treats.
7. Think of social, political, cultural or educational ideas that were reinforced around you as you were growing up. How do they reflect on who you are today?
8. Name the place where your childhood memories are kept: realistically (photo album, diaries, boxes) and metaphorically (branches of a tree, shady porch).
9. Think about the beginning and ending of your poem: where you are from, who you are, where you are going.

Now you have a manuscript that can be easily turned into a book.

Alma Flor Ada

References

Ada de Zubizarreta, A. F. (1964). *Ortografía Práctica*. Lima, Perú: Editorial Arica.

Alma de Zubizarreta. (1969). *Pedro Salinas: El diálogo creador*. Madrid: Gredos. (Colección Románica Hispánica.) (2018) *Pedro Salinas: El diálogo creador*. Mariposa Transformative Education.

Ada, A. F. (   ) "La enseñanza bilingüe a la población hispánica de los Estados Unidos: Condiciones presentes, posibilidades futuras." In Miguel Siguán (Ed.) *Enseñanza en dos lenguas y resultados escolares*. IX Seminario sobre "Educación y lenguas." Universidad de Barcelona p.73-84

Ada, A. F. (1987) "Creative Education for Bilingual Teachers". In M. Ogazawa-Rey, J. Anderson, and R. Traver (Eds.) *Teachers, Teaching, and Teacher Education*. Cambridge, MA: Harvard Educational Review. Reprint Series No. 19, 57-65.

Ada, A. F. (1988). "The Pájaro Valley experience: Working with Spanish-speaking parents to develop children's reading and writing skills through the use of children's literature." In T. Skutnabb-Kangas & J. Cummins (eds.), *Minority education: From shame to struggle.* Clevendon, England: Multilingual Matters.

Ada, A. F. (1998) "Creative Reading: A relevant methodology for language minority children." In Catherine Walsh   (Ed.) *Literacy as Praxis: Culture, Language and Pedagogy.* Norwood, NJ: Ablex.

Ada, A. F. (2003)0. A *magical encounter: Latino children's literature in the classroom*, 2nd ed. Boston: Allyn & Bacon.
(2016) 3ra ed. San Rafael, CA: Mariposa Transformative Education.

Ada, A. F. (2007) "A Lifetime of Learning to Teach" in *Journal of Latinos and Education,* vol 6, number 2.

Adam A. F. & Beutel, C. (1993). *Participatory Research as a Dialogue for Social Action.* Unpublished

Manuscript. University of San Francisco.

Ada, A. F. & Campoy, F. I. (2004). *Authors in the classroom: A transformative education process.* Boston: Pearson Education, Allyn & Bacon.

Ada, A. F. & Campoy, F. I. (2015). *Está linda la mar: Para entender la poesía y usarla en el aula.* A book on the use of poetry in the classroom. Santillana / Vista Higher Learning.

Ada, A. F. & Campoy, F. I. (2017). *Música amiga. Aprender cantando.* Mariposa Transformative Education.

Ada, A. F. & Campoy, F. I. (2018). *Palabra amiga. Domina el idioma.* Velázquez Press.

Ada, A. F., Campoy, F. I. & Colin Powell (2018). *Guía para padres y maestros de niños bilingües.* Clevedon, England: Multilingual Matters.

Freinet, C. (1975/1973). *El texto libre.* Barcelona, Spain: Editorial Laia.

Freinet, C. (1976/1974). *El método natural de la lectura.* Barcelona, Spain: Editorial Laia.

Alma Flor Ada

Freinet, C. (1986/1969). *Técnicas Freinet de la escuela moderna*. Mexico City: Siglo XXI Editores.

Freire, P. (1970). *Pedagogy of the oppressed*. New York. Continuum.

Freire, P. (1982). *Education for critical consciousness*. New York: Continuum.

Freire, P. (1997). *Pedagogy of hope: Reliving pedagogy of the oppressed*. New York: Herder and Herder.

Maguire, Patricia (1987). *Doing Participatory Research: a feminist perspective*. The Center for International Education. The University of Massachusetts.

Maturana. H.R & Varela, F. J. (1987). *The tree of knowledge*. Boston: New Science Library.

Sherover-Marcuse, R. (1994). Liberation theory: Axioms and working assumptions about the perpetuation of social oppression. In N. González-Yuen (Ed.), *The politics of liberation*, Dubuque, A: Kendall/Hunt.

Sherover-Marcuse, R. (2000). Collection of writings published posthumously on the web at http://www.unlearningracism.org/writings.htm

Selective Titles of Alma Flor Ada's publications

Children and Young Adults Literature

BOOKS

POETRY

A la sombra de un ala. Madrid. Escuela Española.
Abecedario de los animales. Madrid. Espasa-Calpe.
*Arenas y trinos. Sand and song. Abecedario del río.
        The ABC's of the River.* Houston, TX. Arte
        Público Press.
Arrullos de la sirena. Bogotá. Panamericana.
Coral y espuma. Madrid. Espasa-Calpe.
Días y días de poesía. Carmel, CA. Hampton-Brown.
Gathering the Sun. [A Farmworkers' ABC]. Illust.
        Simón Silva. NY: Harper.
Todo es canción. Loqueleo.
Una vez en el medio del mar. Madrid. Escuela
        Española.

Childhood MEMORIES

Barriletes. NY: Laredo Publishing
Días de circo. NY: Laredo Publishing
Island Treasures. Growing Up in Cuba. NY:
        Atheneum. / *Tesoros de mi isla*. Loqueleo.
Pin, pin, sarabín. NY: Laredo Publishing
Pregones. NY: Laredo Publishing
Under the Royal Palms. NY: Atheneum
        / *Bajo las palmas reales*. Loqueleo.

Where the Flame Trees Bloom. NY: Atheneum. /
     Allá donde florecen los framboyanes. Loqueleo.

NARRATIVE

El manto de plumas. Santillana
El vuelo de los colibríes. NY: Laredo.
Encaje de piedra. Buenos Aires: Editorial
     Guadalupe. / Del Sol Books.
Lugares mágicos. Mariposa.
Me llamo María Isabel. NY: Atheneum
My Name is María Isabel. NY: Atheneum
¿Quién cuida al cocodrilo? Madrid. Espasa.

Co-authored by Gabriel Zubizarreta-Ada.

Con cariño, Amalia. NY: Atheneum
Love Amalia. NY: Atheneum
Dancing Home. . NY: Atheneum
Nacer bailando. NY: Atheneum.

PICTURE BOOKS

Picture Books Series

Cuentos para todo el año. ~Stories the year 'round
Illustrated by Viví Escriba. Loqueleo
Cómo nació el arcoíris   *How the rainbow came to be*
Después de la tormenta *After the Storm*
El papalote   *The Kite*
El susto de los fantasmas   *What are ghosts afraid of?*
La hamaca de la vaca   *In the Cow's Backyard*
La jaula dorada   *The Golden Cage*

La piñata vacía	The Empty Piñata
La sorpresa de Mamá Coneja	
	A Surprise for Mother Rabbit
No fui yo	It Wasn't Me
¡No quiero derretirme!	I don't want to melt
¿Pavo para la Cena de Gracias? No, gracias	
	Turkey for Thanksgiving? No, thanks.
Rosa alada	A Rose with Wings

**Libros para contar. Stories for the Telling
Illustrated by Viví Escriba. Loqueleo**

Amigos	Friends
El canto del mosquito	The Song of the Teene-Tiny Mosquito
Me gustaría tener	How Happy I Would Be
¿Quién nacerá aquí?	Who's hatching Here?
Una extraña visita	Strangely Strange Visitors

Hidden Forest Series – Illustrated by Leslie Tryon

Dear Peter Rabbit. NY: Atheneum
Querido Pedrín. NY: Atheneum
Extra! Extra! Hidden Forest News. NY: Atheneum.
¡Extra! ¡Extra! Noticias del Bosque Escondido.
Loqueleo
Yours truly, Goldilocks. NY: Atheneum.
Atentamente, Ricitos de Oro. Loqueleo
With Love, Little Red Hen. NY: Atheneum.

Individual Bilingual Picture Books

Daniel Mystery Egg + El huevo misterioso. Hartcourt
Daniel's Pet + Daniel y su mascota. Hartcourt
El cuadradito azul + The Little Blue Square. Mariposa.

Let Me Help! / Quiero ayudar. NY: Lee and Low.
Medio pollito / Half-chicken. NY: Doubleday
The Lizard and the Sun / La lagartija y el sol. Illust.
     Felipe Dávalos. NY: Doubleday.

Individual Picture Books with English & Spanish separate editions

Abuelita's Secret. / El secreto de abuelita. Benchmark.
Cristina and the Frog. / Cristina y la rana.   Frog
     Street.
*Había una vez en Dragolandia / Once Upon a Time in
     Dragonland*. Frog Street.
I Love Saturdays… y domingos. NY: Atheneum /
     Me encantan los sábados y domingos. Loqueleo.
In the barrio / En el barrio. Scholastic
*La tataranieta de Cucarachita Martina / The Great-
     Granddaughter of Cucarachita Martina*.
     Scholastic.
The Gold Coin. Illust. Neil Waldman. Atheneum /
     La moneda de oro. Spain: Everest.
*The rooster who went to his uncle's wedding /El gallo
     que fue a la boda de su tío*. Frog Street
The Unicorn of the West/El unicornio del oeste.
     Atheneum.

Individual Titles in English

Abuelita's Secret. Raycraft.
Friend Frog. Lori Lohstoeter. Hartcourt / Scholastic
Jordi's Star. Illust. Susan Gaber. Putnam
Serafina's Birthday. NY: Atheneum
The Malachite Palace. Illust. Leonid Gore. NY:
     Atheneum
The Three Golden Oranges. Illust. Reg Cartwright.
     NY: Atheneum

Individual Titles in Spanish

El pañuelo de seda. NY: Laredo.
El reino de la geometría. NY: Laredo.
El reino feliz. Loqueleo
Lugares mágicos. Mariposa.

CDs of stories read by Alma Flor Ada

produced by Santillana
Cuentos para todo el año + Stories the Year 'round
      Santillana/Loqueleo
produced by Mariposa Tranformative Education
The Gold Coin + La moneda de oro
The Malachite Palace – The Unicorn of the West –
     Jordi's Star

CDs of Alma Flor's poems sang by Suni Paz

produced by Mariposa Tranformative Education
Abecedario
Arrullos de la sirena
Como una flor
Coral y espuma. Abecedario del mar.
Cuéntame un cuento
Gathering the Song [the Spanish poems]
 Todo es canción
Tres princesas

Adult Literature

Novels
A pesar del amor. Madrid: Alfaguara.
A pesar del amor. Mariposa.

En clave de sol. Madrid: Alfaguara.
En clave de sol. Mariposa.

Memoirs
Cartas desde Napoli. Mariposa.
Vivir en dos idiomas. Madrid: Aguilar.
Vivir en dos idiomas. Mariposa.

Poetry
Cuando el amor vive en la mirada. Mariposa.
Minuto eterno. Mariposa.

Literary Analisis
Pedro Salinas. El diálogo creador. Madrid: Gredos.
Pedro Salinas. El diálogo creador. Mariposa.

Pedagogical Works
A Magical Encounter: Latino Children's Literature in the Classroom. 1st edition. Santillana.
2nd Edition Allyn & Bacon.
3rd Mariposa Transformative Education
Alma Flor Ada and You. Volumes I and II. Libraries Unlimited.
My Books. My Life. Mariposa Transformative Education

DVDs -
all produced by Mariposa Transformative
        Education
Creative Reading Methodology
Escribiendo desde el corazón
Hagamos caminos. A Creative Reading Initial Literacy
        Program
La lectura creadora
Meeting an Author
My Journey as a Writer
Participatory Reasearch – A Dialogue with Paulo
        Freire

Publications in Collaboration with F. Isabel Campoy

Children and Young Adults Literature

Poetry & Songs Anthologies

Alegrías. *A poetry program published by National Geographic.*
> A Poetry Anthology containing poems for each day of the year and three Big Books with selected poems, all lavishly illustrated
> More than 200 of the poems have been put to music and all the poems have been read by Alma Flor Ada or F. Isabel Campoy.
> Songs and poems are accessible on the website that also features pedagogical suggestions and the possibility to print all the poems for the students to decorate and create their own anthologies.

En los montes, monte soy. Houghton Mifflin Hartcourt
Poemas con ton y son. Frog Street
Salta, saltarín. Frog Street
Superlibro de rima K. ¡Arriba la lectura! Houghton Mifflin Harcourt
Superlibro de rima 1. ¡Arriba la lectura! Houghton Mifflin Harcourt

Collections

Cielo abierto
> Series de: Cultura. Poesía. Teatro. Libros creados por niños y padres.

Cuentos para celebrar. Twelve individual books in separate editions in English and Spanish to recognize significant days of the year with an original story and non-fiction information.

Música amiga. Ten books with twelve books of poems. And ten accompanying CDs with the poems turned into songs by accomplished composer Suni Paz.

Puertas al sol – Gathering the Sun.
Art. Culture. Biographies. Poetry. Theater Series. Santillana/Loqueleo

NARRATIVE

Ficción

Cuentos que contaban nuestras abuelas. NY: Atheneum.

Semilla de luz. Madrid: Alfaguara.

Semilla de luz. Doral, FL: Santillana.

Tales Our Abuelitas Told. NY: Atheneum.

Ficción + Non-fiction

¡Sí somos latinos! Charlesbridge.

Yes! We Are Latinos. Charlesbridge.

Children's Oral Folklore. Bilingual Books

Mamá Goose. Illust. Maribel Suárez. Hyperion/ Disney

Merry Navidad. Illust. Viví Escrivá. NY: Harper Collins

MuuMoo. Illust. Viví Escrivá. NY: Harper Collins

Pío Peep. Illust. Viví Escrivá. NY: Harper Collins

Ten Little Puppies + Diez Perritos. Illust. Ulises Wensell. NY: Harper Collins.

CDs

produced by Mariposa Tranformative Education

Cuentos que contaban nuestras abuelas. Recorded by
F. Isabel Campoy and Alma Flor Ada
Pío Peep. Recorded by Suni Paz

DvDs

El encuentro mágico con el folklore infantil. Mariposa
Transformative Education.

Pedagogical Works

*Authors in the Classroom. A Transformative Education
Experience.* Allyn & Bacon.
Ayudando a nuestros hijos. Mariposa
Transformative Education.
*Está linda la mar. Para entender la poesía y usarla en la
clase.* Santillana.
*Guía para padres y maestros de niños bilingües. [2nd
edition].* With Colin Baker. Clevedon,
England: Multilingual Matters.
La fascinante historia de la lengua española.
Velázquez Press.
Música amiga: Aprender cantando. Mariposa
Transformative Education.
Owning Meaning. Mariposa Transformative
Education.
Palabra amiga. Domine su idioma. Velázquez Press.
Palabra amiga. Domine su idioma. [Cuaderno de
Ejercicios] Velázquez Press.
Spanish Literacy Startegies for Young Learners.
Frog Street.

Books about the Ada-Lafuente Family
All published by Mariposa Transformative Education

Alma Flor Ada [editor]
> **Dolores Salvador: Maestra de maestras.**
> **Mi cada vez más querida mía** [*letters from Medardo Lafuente a Dolores Salvador.*]

Alma Flor Ada [author]
> **A las orillas del Tínima. Antepasados de la Familia Lafuente Salvador**
> **Casa de grandes arcos. Dos familias luminosas.**
> **Once there were four children** [memories of the childhood of Rosalma, Alfonso, Miguel and Gabriel Zubizarreta Ada]

Alma Lafuente de Ada [author]
> **Del ayer hasta el mañana**
> **Manantial de sentimientos**
> **Mi vida**

Medardo Lafuente [author]
> **Jornadas líricas.** Poems. **[Book 2nd ed.]**
> **Jornadas líricas [CD, read by Alma Flor Ada]**

Mireya Lafuente [author]
> **Recuerdos de mi vida**

Virginia Lafuente [author]
> **Palabras**

Modesto Ada Rey [author]
> **Sin temor de Dios. Hacer el bien por el**
> **bien mismo.**

Rosalma Zubizarreta Ada [author]
> **Dinamic Facilitation. From Conflict to**
> **Creative Collaboration.**
> **La facilitación dinámica. Del conflicto a la**
> **colaboración creativa.**